CHRISTIAN TRAININ

BEING A CHRISTIAN LEADER

A Guide to Leading Church Organisations and Committees

Fred Bacon

Illustrations by June Gascoigne

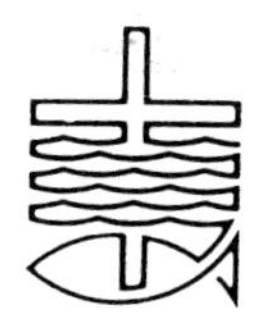

Published by
The Baptist Union of Great Britain
September 1990

ISBN 0 901472 14 X

Designed, typeset and produced for the Baptist Union of Great Britain by Gem Publishing Company, Brightwell, Wallingford, Oxfordshire.

Printed in Great Britain by Pike Printers, Kettering, Northamptonshire.

CONTENTS

PREFACE

This manual on *Being a Christian Leader* has been prepared with the aim of meeting several needs.

CTP COURSE

It may be that you are planning to use this manual as part of the Christian Training Programme Diploma Course. If so, you will need to work your way through the units with the guidance and encouragement of your tutor, completing the assignments which are found at the end of Units 2, 4, 6 and 8. The various exercises, To Think About sections and Group Training Course material will hopefully stimulate and interest you, but you will be assessed only on your response to those four assignments.

GROUP TRAINING COURSE

The material has also been prepared for use by a church based group or perhaps in a training course arranged by a group of churches or a Baptist Association.

The suggested agendas for eight sessions, together with further details and explanations about using the material in a group training context will be found starting on Page 76. **A handbook for leaders of group training courses** is available from the CTP office at Baptist House, 129 Broadway, Didcot, Oxon.

PERSONAL INTEREST AND STUDY

There will be others who are neither working on a CTP course nor part of a group, but who have an interest in this subject. This manual will prove valuable if you are a leader in your church or believe God may be calling you into some role of leadership.

TO TAKE YOU FURTHER

The deliberate aim of this manual is to be general. It assumes that leaders of specific groups in local churches will want to go further and avail themselves of any specialist training designed for people in their particular leadership positions.

For example, youth leaders will find valuable help in *Spectrum*, the inter-church training programme for youth workers published by the NCEC and sponsored by the Baptist Union Youth Office. Leaders in uniformed youth organisations have national programmes of training provided for them. Deacons and church officers would be helped by material on church administration published by the author of this manual. The Baptist Union CTP also has material on church administration. Resources for those involved in leadership among women may be obtained from the Womens' Office at the BU in Didcot. For Sunday school/junior church/Bible class leaders, a course is available called *Equipped to Teach*. Further details can be had from the Education Office at the BU.

In Appendix B (Page 101) several books are mentioned which are either referred to in the manual or will offer you further material on the themes considered. There are also names and addresses of some organisations offering training or providing resources for churches to set up their own training courses.

The author has written three workbooks to assist churches in their life and mission. The titles are *Planning Your Church's Programme, Making the Most of People's Resources,* and *Getting Well Organised.* These workbooks fill out several themes in this manual and the sample documents in Appendix C are taken from the workbooks. Details about where these workbooks can be obtained are on page 101.

Paul Mortimore
Editor

AUTHOR'S PREFACE

This manual is designed to help Christian leaders *and* potential leaders discover the principles and practice of leadership in church organisations and committees, and then apply them in action.

The terms 'leaders' and 'potential leaders' cover a wide group of people. 'Leaders' means any who are involved in running, or helping to run, church organisations or serve on committees. 'Potential leaders' means those who are already inclined to — or can be persuaded to — prepare themselves to serve in leadership positions.

The following are examples of the organisations and committees the course is designed to cover:

Organisations	**Committees**
Children's Club	Catering
Choir/Music Group	Christian Education
Luncheon Club	Diaconate
Men's Club	Fabric
Mothers and Toddlers Group	Finance
Pastoral Care Group	Missions
Play Group	Pastoral Care
Sunday School (under various names)	Publicity
Uniformed organisations	Worship
Women's Meetings (of various titles)	Youth Council
Youth Club	
Youth Fellowship (or whatever called)	

(We shall mostly use the term 'organisation' to cover both organisations and committees.)

You may belong to a church which is so small that it has very few organisations. But it can still be worth your training for leadership. You may be asked to set up an organisation or committee in your church or, if your church expands and more organisations and committees are established, you can be the source of useful advice and help. Or, again, you may move some day to another church and be able to use there what you have learnt.

UNIT 1

Setting the Scene

AIM: To enable you to see that leaders are necessary, need choosing carefully and appointing formally if the best leadership for Christ's Church is to be provided.

Sections covered:

A. What is leadership?
B. The need for leadership.
C. Leadership (of a kind) usually emerges.
D. Secure the best leaders.

A. WHAT IS LEADERSHIP?

When we try to define 'leadership' we may feel like the boy who, when asked to define a vacuum, replied, 'Well sir, I've got it in my head but I can't express it!' Nevertheless, the attempt should be made.

It is most difficult if we think of leadership simply in the abstract. But even if we do relate it to practical situations, it remains impossible to find an all-embracing definition that is adequate to cover all. Leadership varies from one situation to another. For instance, leadership is different among children from among adults; it is different in the army from in the church; different at home from in business; different in politics from in a football team.

> ***TO THINK ABOUT . . .***
> **What is your definition of 'leadership'? How does your definition correspond to definitions in standard dictionaries? Look under 'lead'.**

Within the context of this manual we shall confine ourselves to this definition:

> **Leadership in the church situation is: Motivating and enabling others by guidance, discussion, persuasion, example and organisation to follow a line of action.**

This may be imperfect but we shall take is as a sufficient definition for our purposes.

B. *THE NEED FOR LEADERSHIP*

1. TO AVOID CHAOS

Lack of leadership can lead to chaos. Just imagine an open Youth Club without a leader; a Sunday School class without a teacher; or a Church Meeting without a chairman! Have a look at Judges 17:6. Enough said?!

Leadership is needed, however, not only for negative but also positive reasons.

2. TO GET THINGS DONE

From the definition of leadership above it is evident that without leadership little, if anything, worthwhile will be done. We can see this to be true when a church organisation loses its leader and no other can be found; the organisation often soon packs up.

Recall also how, after the Holy Spirit came on the disciples at Pentecost and they were equipped to take the Gospel to 'all the world', Peter saw that someone was immediately needed to take the lead and explain to the crowds what was going on (Acts 2:14). It seems likely that the rest of the apostles also soon became leaders in various spheres. Human groups need leadership if anything positive is to be achieved.

C. *LEADERSHIP (OF A KIND) USUALLY EMERGES*

Although chaos may reign within a group of people, it will be short-lived if action is called for. Some sort of leadership will emerge. If at a large meeting, for example, someone asks the people to move the chairs to face in a different direction and gives no specific guidance how to do it, for a while there is chaos; then some person or persons will take the initiative and try to get co-operation from the rest. Just stand back and watch it happen. Or watch a group of children at play and see how leadership emerges, even if it is transitory and does not stay with the same child all the time.

But although leadership emerges, it may not be the best to achieve the desired results. Some of us have seen situations where the wrong leadership has 'taken over' with disastrous consequences. It happened in the New Testament church with Diotrephes. Look up 3 John 9 to see how John dealt with that disaster.

TO THINK ABOUT . . .
What situations can you recall in which 'wrong' leaders have emerged? Why do you think this happened and what were the consequences?

D. SECURE THE BEST LEADERS

All a church's organisations and committees exist, or should do, for a purpose – God's purpose. It follows, therefore, that they need leaders and the most suitable that can be found. This was certainly so in the early church. God wanted, for instance, the Gospel to be taken to the Gentiles and needed the best possible leaders to do it. So, under the guidance of the Spirit, Paul and Barnabas were set aside at Antioch to begin the task (Acts 13:1–3). It is not surprising that they then practised this principle in the churches they founded. Look at Acts 14:23 to see this point illustrated.

If a church, therefore, is to discover God's will, if it is to be ready and enabled by the Holy Spirit to serve as the body of Christ, that church needs to give careful and prayerful thought as to how best to secure its leaders. We shall deal with this in some detail throughout the Manual. For the moment we pin-point four basic factors to bear in mind in ensuring that the best leaders – of God's appointment – are selected.

1. THE NATURAL LEADER

Often it is the so-called natural leader – the one who naturally finds him or herself directing others – who emerges. But the natural leader is not necessarily the most suitable. If a fire breaks out and few know where the emergency exits are, the natural leader may lead us in the wrong direction, *thinking* it is the right way!

2. THE COMPETENT LEADER

Whom would you rather follow, the person who has natural leadership ability or the person who has knowledge and skill and therefore the competence to succeed?

> ***TO THINK ABOUT . . .***
> **What is your answer?**
> **From your experience think of examples which bear out or contradict the principle expressed in the following quotation.**

Field-Marshal Montgomery wrote in his *Path to Leadership:*

> I reckon that soldiers will be more likely to follow a leader in whose military knowledge they have confidence, rather than a man with much greater personality but with not the same obvious knowledge of his job.

The ideal, of course, is to find leaders in whom both natural leadership ability and competence combine. In 1 Samuel we see that King Saul was obviously a *natural* leader, but what a mess he made of things! On the other hand, in 2 Samuel we see that David, with all his faults, proved to be both a *natural* and a very *able* leader and brought the state of Israel to the peak of its political success.

But people possessing both these qualifications are not necessarily available. If we have to choose, most of us would agree with Lord Montgomery's soldiers and be led by those who both know what is needed to achieve the objectives, and have the ability to succeed. It follows, therefore, that we need to –

3. MAKE CAREFUL SELECTION AND FORMAL APPOINTMENTS

Unfortunately, the person with competence:

- may be too diffident to come forward,
- is overwhelmed by someone with a strong personality, and/or
- is not recognised by the people as having the necessary abilities.

Thus in any organisation there needs to be a system for making the right choice of leaders, who then need appointing formally so that all know to whom they should look for leadership. Consider, for example, the selection and appointment of 'The Seven' in Acts 6:1–6.

Overwhelmed by someone with a strong personality.

> ***TO THINK ABOUT . . .***
> **How were these principles implemented in the appointment of 'The Seven'?**

Such official selection and formal appointment give the quieter but competent leaders the authority to exercise their leadership. As a consequence, recognition is received from those being led and the leaders' confidence is strengthened.

There are other factors which determine who are most suitable as leaders and we shall consider these later. But it should be obvious by now that making the right choice and appointment is crucial if the work of Christ in a church is to go forward as it should.

> ***TO THINK ABOUT . . .***
> **What features can you identify in the following episode which illustrate the points made so far in Sections B, C, and D?**
>
> On a motorway an accident occurred in which a lorry and a car were involved.
>
> Because of the obstruction caused there was considerable danger from and to overtaking traffic. Someone bravely, but rather officiously, tried to direct the traffic past the danger zone but obviously did not understand how to do this and only added to the confusion. He was soon supplanted by someone who clearly knew better how to do it, and with better results. But even he was at times ignored by careless or selfish motorists.
>
> Soon, however, the police arrived. They took over the control of the traffic and the oversight of the situation generally. The motorists then obeyed directions and order was secured.

4. 'BEST' MEANS BEST – NOT NECESSARILY THE IDEAL

Asking for the best available leaders does not mean that we have to wait for the perfect ones. If we do, we shall wait forever. In fact, we can discourage some fine potential leaders if we give the impression that only the ideal is acceptable. It may be, at times, that there just is no suitable and willing person available for a position. In that case the organisation may have to lapse. But God does call and use inadequate people (that's all of us!) and works wonders through them.

TO THINK ABOUT . . .
What examples can you recall from the Bible which illustrate this point?

Nevertheless, we shoud seek the best leadership available. This would be true for a purely secular organisation and must, therefore, be essential for Christ's Church. After all, we are his body through which he is working to further his Kingdom – his rule – in the world. He wants the most dedicated, spiritual, co-ordinated, efficient and effective body possible – only the best is good enough for God. We have to do our utmost, therefore, to ensure that a church begins by choosing and appointing the best leaders that can be found.

How this can be done needs spelling out in some detail. There are other steps necessary to ensure that the leaders are the best that they can be, but that will come later.

Finally, this should be said now in case of misunderstanding. What follows in this course does not provide rigid rules but rather guidelines for your own church to adapt to its own situation.

EXERCISE

The following is an imaginary case for you to study in relation to leading church organisations and committees. It has been designed to include (plenty of) faults and deficiences in the way leadership is practised.

Go through it carefully, noting what you judge to be those faults or deficiencies. Place numbers (starting with 1) in the text at the points where you detect any defect (an example is given in the text in respect of defect 1). Then at the bottom of the text or on a separate sheet of paper describe briefly each fault or deficiency, numbering your comments to correspond with those in the text (see example at end of text).

(At the conclusion of the course you will be asked to repeat the Exercise and compare your answers then with those you give now, noting how what you have learnt is reflected in your later judgement.

The minister of a church sees in his Sunday congregation a young fellow whom he recognises as having been attending for a few weeks. 'We ought to try and use him in the church somehow,' he says to himself during the offertory. 'How can we do it?' he wonders.[1] 'Perhaps the youth club could do with an assistant leader, I'll ask him afterwards. He may even join the church as a result.'

So, after the service he approached him and asked if he would be assistant youth club leader. 'Yes, if you like,' was the reply. 'When should I start?' 'Oh, go along tomorrow night at seven and tell them I've sent you. What's your name, by the way?' 'Don,' he was told.

Don went home to his wife who had been looking after the children and told her that he was going to help at the church Youth Club.

Along he went on Monday night at 7pm. He found that things were not quite as he had imagined. A crowd of teenage boys were larking about around the locked door of the church hall; but there was no leader or staff. This, they said, was usual.

After ten minutes the leader and a helper did appear. 'What are you doing here?' Don was abruptly asked. When he explained, he received a frosty mumbled response. By now the youngsters were running riot in the hall, whereupon the leader took one by the ear and bawled at him and the others to 'Shut up'. After he had obtained some sort of order by shouts and threats the leader set up a few dilapidated games tables and did his best to get the members occupied.

Don and the two young helpers (another had now arrived) all offered to help, but were simply left standing around while the leader continued his crude and not very successful efforts to maintain order.

When closing time arrived and the young people had gone, the two young helpers inquired, 'Didn't we agree to have a staff committee meeting to consider future plans for the club?' 'Oh, well, if we must,' was the response, 'though I don't see much point'. With no formal opening, minutes of a previous meeting or agenda, he launched into an attack on 'them' – meaning mainly the minister and deacons. 'They never come and see what's happening, nor ask me,' he accused. 'Mark you, I wouldn't want them anyway. All I do this for is to get some experience so that the local authority will take me on as a youth leader.' After some aimless talk about the future they went home.

At the next Deacons Meeting someone, under 'Any Other Business', raised the question of the youth club. This led to heated discussion, with various complaints being levelled against the club and especially the leader, though no one knew enough about the situation at first hand to be sure which complaints were true and which untrue. The diaconate decided eventually that unless there was better order in the club within a month it would be closed down and that the church secretary should write and inform the Leader of this decision.

The letter was so ambiguous, however, that the leader thought that he was being dismissed but that the club was to continue. This produced a violent response, whereupon the church secretary wrote again more clearly.

The church secretary received a reply to say that when the leader was asked to take the job on, they had said he could do it indefinitely, and he was going to carry on as long as he wanted, whatever they said . . .

FAULTS AND DEFICIENCIES DETECTED

1. The minister was not following any sensible procedure in making appointments.

UNIT 2

What the Bible Says

AIM: To introduce you to the principles, deduced from the New Testament, which should govern the way church organisations are led.

A. Leadership is necessary.
B. Leaders should have the right aims.
C. Leadership should be adapted to the needs of the situation.
D. The leader is to be a servant.
E. Leadership by a team is preferable.
F. Leaders should be carefully selected.

INTRODUCTION

The methods by which any organisation is run will depend on certain factors relevant to that particular organisation. Take, for instance, a private, commercial airline. The factors which govern the way it runs are as follows:

- it exists to transport passengers and freight; that makes the management of it different from, say, that of an aircraft museum!
- it must make a profit because it is not subsidised
- its staff is paid, not voluntary
- it has an organisational structure in which each employee is under the authority of someone 'higher up' and cannot do just as he or she pleases.

These are all simple and obvious factors, but they are fundamental. Taking account of them will mean that the airline functions in a different area of life and in a different way from, say, a hospital. Basic factors govern actions.

A Christian church, and each part of it, needs to know the basic factors which should govern the way it is run. In the case of a church these are best termed 'principles' because they are more fundamental than 'factors'. We need to ask, therefore, before we go any further what are the principles which should govern the purpose and practice of leadership in a Christian church. It is to the Bible we turn to discover them.

> ***TO THINK ABOUT . . .***
> **Is it realistic to turn to the Bible to discover principles for effective leadership in a local church today? Why do you answer as you do?**

A. LEADERSHIP IS NECESSARY

We partly dealt with this point in Unit 1. We underline it here by adding more illustrations of leadership in the early church.

Jesus set his seal on the necessity of leadership by appointing the Twelve as his closest disciples (Mark 3:13–19) and then, later, commissioning them to be the main leaders – apostles – in the very early days of the church (Matthew 28: 16–20; Acts 1:2, 8). And so, no doubt, they were, though we hear no more about most of them after Acts 8:1.

But after Pentecost twelve leaders were not sufficient, so the Seven were appointed (Acts 6: 1–6). Then later James, the Lord's brother, was recognised as leader in the 'mother' church of Jerusalem in place of Peter (Acts 12:17; 15:13) and, in addition, elders were appointed (Acts 11:30). As other churches were founded, so they had leaders; for example Acts 13:1 – prophets and teachers; Acts 14:23; 20:17 – elders; Philippians 1:1 – bishops and deacons. And so we could go on.

The Disciples – commissioned to be leaders in the early church.

There is no doubt that the New Testament makes plain the necessity of leadership in general and in the local church in particular. It is true, of course, that local churches didn't have the various organisations we have today – unless the Seven were the first 'Pastoral Care Group'. But it is obvious that the New Testament gives the same recognition to their leadership as to more obvious leadership roles in the church.

B. *LEADERS SHOULD HAVE THE RIGHT AIMS*

If you don't know where you are supposed to be going you are not likely to get there! We are not likely to achieve much that is worthwhile if we have no aim in life; nor are we likely to achieve much for Christ if we do not know what our Christian service is for – what our aim is.

Jesus knew his aim; he expressed it in various forms, but a familiar one is John 10:10, 'I have come that they may have life, and have it to the full'. Another clear statement of Jesus' aim is: 'My meat is to do the will of him who sent me' (John 4:34).

> ***TO THINK ABOUT . . .***
> **What aims for life did Jesus resist when he was tempted in the wilderness? See Matthew 4: 1–11.**

Jesus gave his disciples an aim before he left them: 'Go and make disciples of all nations . . .' (Matthew 28:19, 20). Paul was given an aim – to take the Gospel mainly to the Gentiles (Acts 9: 15; Romans 11:13). In the same way we should not accept any opportunity of service without knowing the aim.

So, a leader of a church organisation or member of a committee should be able to say what is:

1. THE AIM OF THE ORGANISATION OR COMMITTEE

Put simply, what is the leader trying to help the organisation or committee achieve? This aim should have been given to it by the church to which it belongs. For example, the aim of a church organisation for younger women called Midweek Special might be expressed as:

> To arrange activities which women of the congregation will attend, but which will also attract those who have no church connection, with the hope that they will eventually be helped to a faith in Christ.

Or that of the church Mission Committee might be:

> To stimulate, harness, and unify support in prayer and giving for mission at home and overseas, and in particular that of the denomination.

2. THE AIM OF THE CHURCH TO WHICH THE ORGANISATION BELONGS

A church organisation is not a separate entity. It has a responsibility to the church of which it is a part and should contribute to the church's aim. Therefore every leader needs to know the church's aim.

What *is* the God-given aim of Christ's church – whether it be the universal Church or a local church? Christians do not always agree on an answer. Nevertheless more and more are accepting that the picture of outstanding significance in the New Testament is that of the body of Christ with each Christian a vital member of it. Romans 12:4, 5 and 1 Corinthians 12:27 emphasise this picture.

The implication is that just as our bodies enable us to do what we wish, and just as Jesus used his physical body to do what he wished, so now his aim is to use his church as his body to fulfil his wishes in the world.

The body of Christ . . . each Christian a vital member of it.

The church's aim could be described, therefore, as:

> To be the body of Christ in order to extend the Kingdom of God in the world.

Unfortunately the church does not always obey him, but all Christians should accept it as Christ's aim for his church and seek to play their parts in his body.

TO THINK ABOUT . . .
Write down in two sentences what you think should be the aim of your church. How can the rich variety in your church — represented by people of differing age, circumstances and experience — help to fulfil that aim?

3. THE AIM OF THE LEADER WITHIN THE CHURCH

TO THINK ABOUT . . .
Before reading on, how would you define your aim as a leader in your church?

In the light of reading the next few paragraphs, check if you want to alter the definition of your aim or alter the author's.

The crucial scripture passage for an answer is Ephesians 4:11, 12 –

> 'And these were his [Christ's] gifts: some to be apostles, some prophets, some evangelists, some pastors and teachers, to equip God's people for work in his service, to the building up of the body of Christ' (New English Bible).

The aim then of Christian leaders is 'to equip God's people for work in his service, to the building up of the body of Christ'. Of course, the leaders spoken of in verse 11 are not, strictly speaking, leaders of church organisations in the present-day sense of the word; in those days they rarely, if ever, had any such organisations. But we can assume that all leaders in a church today should have the same aim.

Therefore, we might describe the aim of the leaders of church organisations as:

> To encourage people to a commitment to Christ and his church and then to equip them for Christian service and so build up the body of Christ.

What will this mean in practice for the organisation leader or committee member? The first sixteen verses of Ephesians 4 make it plain that there are three features they should seek to develop:

- **The numerical growth of the body**. Those who seek to build up the body of Christ will want to win as many as possible to faith in him and lead them into the church.
- **The spiritual strength of the body**. This is in order that members become as serviceable as possible in Christ's hands.
- **The unity of the body**. This means co-ordinating the service of individuals, organisations and committees so as to make the church a united body, usable under Christ's directions. Sadly some organisations get led away from this goal as though they had only themselves to think of. But this is contrary to Christ's intention.

TO THINK ABOUT . . .

'Who aimeth at the sky
Shoots higher much than
he that means a tree'

What does this quotation from George Herbert suggest to you about the importance of having clear aims for the organisation you lead, your church and yourself as a leader?

C. LEADERSHIP SHOULD BE ADAPTED TO THE NEEDS OF THE SITUATION

Some think that the New Testament provides an exact blue-print for what we should do in our local churches today. But when we look closely at the Acts and the Epistles it is patently obvious that there was a wide variety of practices. The leadership patterns mentioned in Section A. above illustrate this clearly.

We can legitimately conclude that the reason for this variation was that the early Christians saw the need, under the guidance of the Holy Spirit, to adapt their practices to the needs of each situation so that the Gospel could have the greatest impact.

We need to follow that principle too, not thinking that there is only one pattern of church life in the New Testament, but being open to the leading of the Spirit, flexible in attitude and ready to adapt our practices to the needs of our church. Unfortunately the church, after New Testament times, became rigid and inflexible in its leadership pattern and it took the Reformation to change it. But thank God the church today is becoming more open than it was to change and diversity. We need wisely to encourage it.

TO THINK ABOUT . . .

In what ways is this happening to the good in your own church?

D. THE LEADER IS TO BE A SERVANT

Every Christian exists to be a servant of God and of others (Philippians 2:5–7), and Christian *leaders* are not exempt. Indeed Jesus went out of his way to stress this to the Twelve. For instance, when James and John were pressurising him for the chief places in his Kingdom, he brought them down to earth by telling them that those who wanted to be *great* had to act as *servants* (Mark 10:35–45).

'We want you to do for us whatever we ask.'

> ***TO THINK ABOUT . . .***
> **What ambitions did these two brothers have? What unworthy ambitions can prompt people to want to be leaders?**

At first sight it appears almost a contradiction to say that a leader should be a servant! – but not if we look at it a little more closely. A person will be both a leader and a servant if leading in order to serve. Service, in other words, must be the purpose of leading and this must govern the attitude towards the task and the people being led.

We can see this more clearly if we consider what it means in practice, first positively (what a leader *will* do) and then negatively (what a leader *will not* do).

1. SERVANT LEADERS WILL:

a. Some times:

- Use strong persuasion.
- Take decisions by themselves.
- Give orders firmly.

In fact, the best service a leader can give is to lead as well as possible and not be like the minister who admitted that the way he led his flock was to see which way they were going and then get in front!

Jesus never said that the Twelve were not to act as leaders but rather that they were to act from the right motive and with the right attitude – that of giving service.

b. At all times:

- Listen carefully.
- Seek the good of others.
- Want to give more than to receive (Matthew 20: 28).
- Continue even though –
  they receive no benefits,
  their work is not acknowledged,
  it brings criticism and hardship (Matthew 20: 28),
  it involves the menial task (John 13: 12–17).
- Step down if it is for the good of the Kingdom.

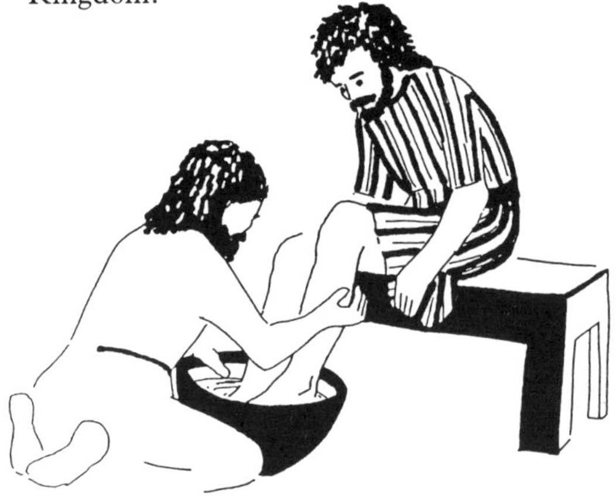

'I have set you an example.'

TO THINK ABOUT . . .
In what practical and relevant ways could the principle of feet-washing be applied today?

2. SERVANT LEADERS WILL NOT:

- Seek their own greatness.
- Be dictatorial.
- Try to satisfy the urge for power or position (1 Peter 5:3).
- Endeavour to control every detail of the organisation instead of delegating responsibilities and authority.
- Resent those who are more competent than themselves.

So leaders will lead, but lead in order to serve. This is a very high ideal; none of us will reach it without God's help, but it is an ideal for all leaders to aim at.

TO THINK ABOUT . . .
What are your reactions to the opening words of the nineteenth-century hymn 'Gentle Jesus, meek and mild'?
What hymns or songs describe adequately the qualities of Jesus as a leader?

E. LEADERSHIP BY A TEAM IS PREFERABLE

The biblical references in Section A. above illustrate that in New Testament days leadership in the church was by a team, except in the case of Diotrephes, and he was a disaster (3 John 9)!

Circumstances, of course, can force a church or organisation to manage with one leader. But this is never ideal.

Here are some of the advantages of team leadership:

- A wider spectrum of people's gifts and abilities are used.
- Fellowship is generated.
- Leaders receive mutual support.
- Work is shared.
- Potential leaders are developed.
- The absence of one team member does not create extreme problems.
- Decision-making is improved.
- Changes in the church are more readily accepted because they are introduced by a group and not just by an individual.
- A succession of leaders is available.

Here are some of the dangers. Team leadership can:

- Give rise to conflict.
- Slow-up decision-making and action.
- Increase administration.

But the positive benefits outweigh the dangers. So for the reasons above we can see why the early church practised team leadership and why, if possible, we should do so today.

TO THINK ABOUT . . .
What further advantages and dangers of team leadership can you think of?

F. LEADERS SHOULD BE CAREFULLY SELECTED

This point was made in Section D. of Unit 1. Now we see that Scripture emphasises it.

Jesus made a calculated selection of the Twelve. He did not ask for volunteers; they were chosen carefully and, according to Luke 6:12–16, prayerfully.

> ***TO THINK ABOUT . . .***
> **Look at these verses. Knowing what you do of the Twelve, who instinctively would you not have chosen as an apostle or potential leader?**
>
> | | |
> |---|---|
> | **Simon (Peter)** | **Matthew** |
> | **Andrew** | **Thomas** |
> | **James** | **James (son of Alphaeus)** |
> | **John** | **Simon (the Zealot)** |
> | **Philip** | **Judas (son of James)** |
> | **Bartholomew** | **Judas Iscariot** |
>
> **What do you learn from the mixture of background and personality represented by the Twelve?**

The Seven, who daily distributed the food to the needy, were not just people who happened to be free and willing. We might think that because the job was 'only administrative' the qualifications needed were not high. Not a bit of it; look again at Acts 6:1–6. And in other accounts of leaders being appointed we see the same kind of care exercised.

> ***TO THINK ABOUT . . .***
> **Look up these examples and consider how this principle is at work: Acts 13:1–3, 14:23; 1 Timothy 3:1–13; Titus 1:5–9.**

We should not imagine that these examples set out a specific pattern which we must rigidly follow; indeed they illustrate the point made in Section C. above that methods varied according to the circumstances. So, we also should adopt the method which is best for the situation in which we are involved.

But we see a principle which should govern our practice: leaders should be carefully selected. That will mean first and foremost prayerfully seeking the leading of the Spirit and then utilising the best procedures which obtain today so that the wisest, God-directed choices are made. We shall consider this further in Unit 7.

> ***TO THINK ABOUT . . .***
> **Does your church appoint its leaders on the basis of who volunteers or whom the church discerns is gifted and called for the tasks? Is there necessarily a difference?**

ASSIGNMENT 1

Imagine you are in a small group discussing the subject of 'Leadership in the local church'. The opinions below are expressed. How would you respond to each one in the light of what has been said in Units 1 and 2 (use a maximum of 150 words for each answer)?

1. **'God is our leader, we don't need human ones.'**
2. **'If God wants leaders he'll make sure we get them without any help from us.'**
3. **'I think the best leaders are those that volunteer when the need arises.'**
4. **'If we are led by the Spirit we won't need to think about having aims for our church or anything else.'**
5. **'We should model our church in every detail on the New Testament church.'**
6. **'I think there should be no leaders at all, after all we are supposed to *serve* each other.'**
7. **'I'm sure a one-man band is the best leadership for getting things done.'**

INTRODUCTION TO UNITS 3 TO 6

In the next four Units we consider leaders' responsibilities, i.e. their functions or responsibilities as leaders of church organisations and members of committees. In Unit 3 we shall deal with these functions in relation to *church organisations and committees* (we shall usually use the term 'organisation' to cover both); in Units 4–6 in relation to the people with whom leaders work – both those within their team and members of the organisation/committee.

In the space available we cannot describe what leaders should do in every kind of organisation; these differ so much. For example, the way the Sunday School should be run will not apply to the Women's Fellowship or the church's Pastoral Care Group. Nevertheless, there are similarities common to all situations and, therefore, we can say in general terms what the function of organisation leaders should be.

UNIT 3

Leaders' Responsibilities

AIM: To understand more clearly what is required of leaders in relation to their church, its organisations and committees, in order to:

A. Foster maximum unity within the church.
B. Help achieve the aim and objectives of the church and the particular organisations or committees.
C. Work within the structures and practices of the church.
D. Plan ahead.
E. Ensure efficient administration.
F. Regularly review how the organisations are functioning.

INTRODUCTION

Organisation in general and organisations in particular are important. Some people disparage them and speak as though the less organisation we have the more God is honoured. The fact is that God himself is the greatest of organisers.

We see it in creation. The sun rises exactly on time each day; the seasons follow each other without fail; we have bodies and minds which are marvellous in the way they are constructed and organised.

We see it too in our redemption. God sent Jesus 'in the fullness of time' (Galatians 4:4). The Bible speaks of the church as being the 'body of Christ' which signifies that the church should try to be as well organised as a healthy human body. So we must not think slightingly of organisation, because God does not.

Organisation, of course, is useless if it has no life in it. A yacht can be perfectly rigged, but until the wind fills the sails it will remain stationary. A church can be organised up to the hilt and yet achieve little unless the breath of the Spirit blows through it. Yet the Spirit can work more effectively in churches where the organisation is good, just as a yacht will take better advantage of the wind if its sails are well set.

So, it is right and proper for us to see what leaders need to do – what responsibilities they have – in order to make their church and its organisations as effective as possible.

A yacht will take better advantage of the wind if its sails are well set.

A. FOSTER MAXIMUM UNITY WITHIN THE CHURCH

It is surprising how some church organisations and committees 'do their own thing', as though they had no responsibilities to the church as a whole. Yet they are glad to make use of the premises, facilities and support which the church provides. Sometimes, unfortunately, this individualism is generated by the indifference or even antipathy of the diaconate and church members towards the organisation.

But a church is supposed to act as the body of Christ, which means that all its parts – limbs – have to work in harmony if it is to be usable by Christ. If the 'limbs', that is the organisations, are unco-ordinated and pulling in different directions, the progress of the church will suffer.

> ***TO THINK ABOUT . . .***
>
> **Consider J.B. Phillips' translation of 1 Corinthians 12:24a–25, 'God has harmonised the whole body . . . that the body should work together as a whole with all the members in sympathic relationship with one another'.**
>
> **Think honestly of ways in which the various parts of your church's life correspond or fail to correspond to the Bible's ideal.**

Fortunately, some churches are well aware that positive action needs to be taken to co-ordinate the work of the church as a whole and enable each section to contribute to its effectiveness. The following are some examples.

a. Different deacons are appointed as link-persons between the diaconate and the various organisations. The deacons are then better able to give advice and support as and when necessary, ensuring that harmony increases.

b. Leaders of organisations are occasionally invited to deacons' and/or church meetings to describe their present situations, share their needs and discuss how mutual help to and from their organisations can be given.

c. Representatives from organisations working in the same area of church life, e.g. youth or women, regularly meet together to share problems and learn from each other. So a church may have a Youth Council (bringing together leaders in the various youth and children's organisations) or a Mission Committee (which acts to promote both home and overseas mission).

Such arrangements can help maximise unity of action, and leaders of organisations should encourage this and co-operate with it.

B. HELP ACHIEVE AIMS AND OBJECTIVES

In this context we shall use the term 'aim' to refer to an overall goal and the term 'objectives' to describe the short-term steps which must be taken to achieve the aim.

Every church and church organisation should have worthwhile aims and then be clear about the objectives by which those aims can be fulfilled. These should be clearly defined and accepted. Merely doing *something* is not necessarily doing what is *best*! You can be busy doing nothing, or busy doing the wrong things. An archer may hit a bulls-eye, but may have aimed at the wrong target!

Whoops!

It is possible to expend an excess of time and effort in a church organisation, but to little or no avail because you have been trying to do second-rate or useless things. Indeed you may be doing positive damage. For instance, the leader of a housegroup might be leading people astray by erroneous teaching and/or setting the people against their church so that hostility and division result. The fact that the leader's aim is being achieved does not make it acceptable, rather the reverse.

Therefore:

1. LEADERS SHOULD ACCEPT AND PROMOTE –

a. The aim of their church

Each church should spell out its aim. (In Unit 2 Section B.2 on page 16 is one possible expression of this.)

b. The aims of their organisations

Each church organisation or committee should also have an expressed aim. If a church has not formulated these for its different organisations, their leaders should badger it until it does; if it still will not do so, leaders should work them out for themselves. (Unit 2 Section B.1, page 15 gives examples.)

The aims of a church and its organisations, as necessary as they are, are only generalisations and do not detail the necessary particular actions which will put those aims into effect. These actions are the objectives.

Therefore:

2. LEADERS SHOULD ACCEPT AND PROMOTE –

a. The objectives of their church

Examples of these are:

- Worship and pray.
- Nurture Christians.
- Unify the membership.
- Encourage and equip Christians for service.
- Evangelise – at home and abroad.
- Give pastoral care.
- Take social action –at home and abroad.
- Relate to other Christians.

> ***TO THINK ABOUT . . .***
> **How would you define the aim and objectives of the church of which you are part?**

b. The objectives of their organisations

Examples of these for the Midweek Special women's organisation referred to in Unit 2 Section B.1 are:

- Provide interest, recreation and fun.
- Stimulate friendly contact with others.
- Encourage a caring concern among the members.
- Enable those who are unfamiliar with church to appreciate the value of the Christian faith and what it can mean to them.
- Introduce them to the life of the church as a whole.

The Kingdom of God will be substantially furthered if a church sets worthwhile aims and objectives for itself and its organisations and if all the leaders accept them and promote them. If any leaders cannot conscientiously accept the declared aims and objectives of their church or organisations they should have the honesty to say so and seek by proper means to change them. If this is impossible, they should find other spheres of service where they can feel at home.

> ***TO THINK ABOUT . . .***
> **What objectives have been agreed in your organisation or committee for the next two months and for the next two years?**

C. *WORK WITHIN THE STRUCTURES AND PRACTICES OF THE CHURCH*

Leaders should not only accept the aims and objectives of their church and its organisations but also work within its declared structures and practices. Of course, no church should try to place an organisation in a strait jacket, unwisely restraining imaginative, enterprising and fruitful action. But there are certain structures and practices within which organisations need to work if they are to contribute to the progress of the church. These vary from denomination to denomination. We speak here only of Baptist churches and of that principle which most determines their structures and practices. It is –

1. CONGREGATIONAL CHURCH GOVERNMENT

In most British Baptist churches it is the members who, under God, have the ultimate authority; the right, that is, to make decisions about what is done in and through the church. In a local Roman Catholic church, for instance, it is the priest who has that ultimate authority. Although he will consult the people and may invite them to make decisions, he can always have the last word if he wishes. Ours is called 'congregational church government' because it is the congregation – the old-time word for the church membership – who always has the final say about what happens. Church members delegate quite a lot of decision-making to the deacons and other leaders, but they still retain the ultimate authority in all matters.

We speak usually of the government of a church where one leader or a small group governs as *authoritarian*; and where the church members govern as *democratic*. 'Democratic' means, 'being governed by the people' – the Greek word 'demos' means 'people'. While, therefore, it is true in one sense that a church is a *demo*cracy this does not alter the fact that a church is, or certainly should be, a *theo*cracy, or ruled by God – 'theos' means 'God'. The church members while using democratic procedures in decision-making are doing so in order to discover God's will. So, God should rule the church, the church members simply act on his behalf.

> ***TO THINK ABOUT . . .***
> **Is the term 'democratic', to describe the government of a local Baptist church, helpful or a hindrance? If the latter, what other term would you choose?**

Here is not the place to give reasons why Baptists and others believe this is the superior form of church government. It is of interest, however, that those main-line churches which are authoritarian in government are increasingly encouraging their people to participate in decision-making.

2. CHURCH ORGANISATION CHART

We can represent the structures in most of our Baptist churches by the Church Organisation Chart opposite. (Note: 'Diaconate' includes 'minister'.)

Baptist churches are increasingly drawing up church rules/guidelines with which organisation leaders should become familiar. If none exist in writing it will be a case of learning from experience what are the structures and practices of the church.

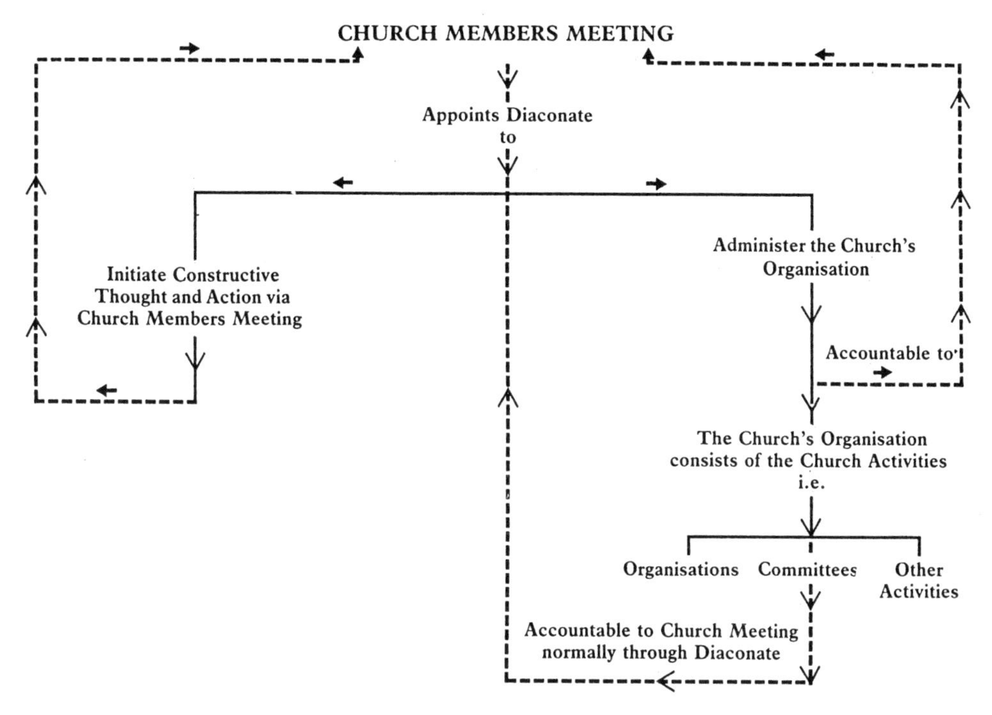

D. PLAN AHEAD

Leaders of every organisation do some planning for the future, if only to fix the date of the next meeting! But that is hardly enough. How easy it is to drift along doing what has been done before simply because it *has* been done before, or just reacting to what circumstances bring. What is needed is long-term planning, carefully and prayerfully thought out.

'I propose we DO meet on 16 December and you two send your apologies.

God is a long-term planner. He planned our salvation from 'the foundation of the world' (Revelation 13:8). He called Abram to be the founder of the nation through which Christ, 2000 years later, was to come (Genesis 12: 1–3). And he has already planned for the climax of history, the perfecting of all things in Christ (Acts 3:20,21; 2 Peter 3:13).

Our commonsense should tell us not to be surprised at this. Therefore we need to make conscious and deliberate efforts to plan our organisation programmes well ahead if we are to make the progress we should.

'Future action' should be an item on the agenda of every organisation's committee meeting and, perhaps once a year, adequate time should be set aside to plan for the twelve months ahead. However, this can probably best be combined with a regular review of the organisation's progress (see Section F below).

TO THINK ABOUT . . .

What aspects of the organisation or committee in which you serve are the results of long term planning?

What do you learn from your answer.

E. ENSURE EFFICIENT ADMINISTRATION

The term 'administration' can have many meanings ranging from the total management of an organisation to the task of putting stamps on letters. Here we use it to mean:

> The responsibilities involved in planning various activities, and the secretarial tasks, office work, financial management, personal contacts and other work involved in implementing the plans.

So, by this definition you are administrating if you organise the Sunday School picnic. This will involve, for instance, booking the venue and the coach, arranging for someone to do the catering, making phone-calls, writing letters, taking money, paying bills, keeping accounts, keeping records for next time, calling the teachers together to discuss matters and keeping them informed.

Sometimes administration is spoken of in disparaging terms as though of little significance. People who talk that way need to think again.

Good administration can make all the difference between success and failure. Some examples will illustrate the point:

- a delayed telephone call means that the venue for the Sunday School picnic is already fully booked
- money unwisely spent means having to forego something crucially important
- a carelessly worded letter means that the coach driver goes to the wrong church
- the notices to parents are not clear, so that they are not there to meet the coach on its return; one little tot is terribly upset and this leads to a dispute which results in her being taken away from Sunday School!

We could go on with examples – some more serious than those above. Good administration is most important and organisation leaders should do their best to see that it is efficiently carried out. The book *Church Administration* contains information which could be of value to organisation leaders. (See Appendix B for details.)

TO THINK ABOUT . . .
Why is it that administration is so often talked about in disparaging terms? Why is it sometimes regarded as less spiritual ministry than other aspects of leadership?

I think I booked the coach for 9.30 . . . or was it 10.30?

F. REVIEW REGULARLY THE ORGANISATION'S FUNCTIONING

When we put a new car on the road, we cannot assume that it will function satisfactorily for the rest of its days without regular checks and servicing. So it is with a church organisation; leaders need to ask from time to time, 'How are we doing?' They then need to make regular reviews and appraisals, and introduce improvements in the light of what is learnt.

> Somehow we have assumed that because our work is being done by volunteer employees, it must therefore be of an inferior quality, and we dare not expect high standards of performance. The result has been the offering to God of shoddy workmanship and programming that does not pass the most elementary tests of adequacy. The Christian organisation should be genuinely interested in quality control. (*Competent to Lead*, K.O. Gangel, *p*125.)

TO THINK ABOUT . . .

Does your church have any means of exercising 'quality control' over its organisations and committees?

If so, is it helpful?

If not, would you welcome such accountability?

How often reviews should be made will depend on circumstances, but they should be *regular*, whether six-monthly, annually, biennially or whatever. A review exercise falls into three main stages:

- **A survey** of the organisation's present situation, with the results tabulated.
- **An appraisal**, based on the results of the survey, of the efficiency and effectiveness of the organisation's activities.
- **Action** to improve its effectiveness – or, if desirable, to disband it.

The methods of 'reviewing' can be shaped to suit the needs of each organisation. One method for the survey is to produce a questionnaire to be completed by the leaders of the organisation or committee. (A sample questionnaire from which leaders could frame their own is found in Appendix C.

A method, commonly practised today in the secular field, which aids *appraisal* and sets targets for *action* to improve performance in the future, is Management by Objectives (MBO). The technique makes review and appraisal easier in that objectives are first set for an organisation or individual. Then, after a set period, a check is made as to how well the objectives have been met. This proves to be a stimulus to progress. MBO can usefully be combined with planning ahead (see Section D. above).

EXERCISE

Draw up a Targets Plan (sample given in Appendix C) for a church's Pastoral Care Group for the next twelve months.

The group was formed three years ago to organise the pastoral care of members (in the widest sense) and, as time permits, of the immediate neighbourhood. It has not, however, come up to expectations and the deacons have initiated a review of its work to culminate in a Target Plan.

Set targets to be met within twelve months, covering the following areas:

1. **To provide a suitable and competent Pastoral Care Group.**
2. **To encourage *spontaneous* pastoral care by the congregation.**
3. **To improve *organised* pastoral care.**

UNIT 4

Pulling Together

AIM: To see more clearly what is required of organisation leaders in relation to the people they work with in order to –

A. Work co-operatively in a team.
B. Adopt the appropriate style of leadership.
C. Meet equally the three areas of need (task, team and individual).
D. Motivate others.

A. WORK CO-OPERATIVELY IN A TEAM

We saw in Unit 2 that teamwork was typical of leadership in New Testament churches and that there is good reason for practising this today. It is interesting, and significant, that we have support for this in the secular field where management teams are more common nowadays than they used to be.

For some church organisations team leadership would be a luxury; in smaller churches one person sometimes has to soldier on alone. But where possible teamwork should be practised. For instance, the typical afternoon 'Women's Fellowship' (or whatever may be its name) has officers; a president/chairperson/leader, secretary, treasurer and perhaps one or two more. They should see themselves as making up a united team, responsible for the effective running of the meeting. This principle should be practised where practicable by other organisations and committees.

For an effective leadership team the following points should be borne in mind:

This approach of leading from among should be more common for all leadership teams than the authoritarian style because, among other things, it better symbolises servant attitudes and is more conducive to Christian fellowship. We shall have more to say below on this question of leadership styles.

With a church committee the chairperson is technically the overall leader, though in practice the secretary often holds the reins of leadership. But whether it is of an organisation or committee, the overall leader, while giving a firm and clear lead, should do so from among rather than in front.

> ***TO THINK ABOUT . . .***
> **What benefits and what potential hazards are there in an overall leader leading from *among* a team?**

1. THE OVERALL LEADER SHOULD:

a. Lead from among the team as far as possible

The role of the overall leader of the team will vary from organisation to organisation. The Scout Troop leader, for example, will tend to be more authoritarian with his assistant leaders than, say, the Sunday School superintendent with the Sunday School teachers. The Sunday School leader/superintendent will tend to be 'first among equals'.

b. Be a 'Player-Manager'.

In footballing terms (s)he will captain the team as a player on the field, not from the touch-line.

c. Inspire and motivate the team to do its job well.

d. Delegate tasks advantageously.

The subject of delegation will be dealt with more fully in Unit 5, Section D. Suffice it to say here that some overall leaders, finding it difficult to share out the work, keep too much to them-

. . . be a player manager.

selves. The result is that they are overworked, less is achieved, and the abilities of others are left unutilised.

e. Help equip the team for its task.

f. Foster the unity of the team.

g. Be a good example of spirituality, high moral standards, competence and pastoral caring.

2. TEAM MEMBERS SHOULD:

a. Be committed to the work of the organisation.

b. Become an integral part of the team.

c. Conscientiously play the part assigned to them.

d. Help the overall leader to play his or her part productively.

e. Be a good example of spirituality, high moral standards, competence and pastoral caring.

B. ADOPT THE APPROPRIATE STYLE OF LEADERSHIP

The style of leadership you adopt will need to vary from time to time, situation to situation, and group to group. It is interesting that, as his letters illustrate, Paul varied his approach to the different churches. He took a firm line, for instance, with churches which he actually founded and where he thought he had the right to speak authoritatively. We see this with the Corinthians whose church he had been instrumental in starting. But in writing to the Romans, whom he had never met, he does not attempt to give directions in quite the same fashion.

So we look now at some of the different styles than can be adopted by leaders.

1. LEADERSHIP STYLES

Some of the terms used for leadership styles are: authoritarian, autocratic, traditional, charismatic, classical, bureaucratic, paternalistic, pastoral, participative, democratic. Some of them are almost identical in meaning. You need not remember all these, but they do show how much variation there is in terminology. We shall confine ourselves to four main styles found in churches.

a. Authoritarian (or autocratic)

This style is seen in the armed forces and in most business firms. The leader tends to be 'the big boss'. In extreme cases the leader makes all the decisions, telling others what to do. Usually (s)he consults others but still has the last word.

Church groups where it exists are mainly the uniformed organisations – Brigades, Scouts, Guides, whose system is based on army discipline – and, to some degree, in youth clubs where the decision-making rests finally with the leaders; though it is good to discover that young people are increasingly being involved in running their own affairs.

> ***TO THINK ABOUT . . .***
> **What are the consequences of a leader making all the decisions in a group or organisation?**
> **Are those consequences good or bad?**

b. Paternalistic (or pastoral)

Here the leader acts as a father/mother figure, treating the people in the organisation rather as a family, caring for them, giving them a sense of security but, while listening to their opinions, tending to make decisions for them. This kind of approach was taken understandably by missionaries in earlier days with tribes where the chief was the father figure. This approach was also common in 'family' firms like Cadbury's and Ford's, where the welfare of the employees was a major concern of the owners. It is now largely out-moded, partly because employees felt themselves to be dependants, too much under the control of their employers. This style continues sometimes, however, in church children's organisations, and – whether it should or not – in meetings for older women.

c. Charismatic

Here the term 'charismatic' relates to the personality of the leader and not to her or his theology or style of worship – it is quite possible to have a charismatic person who is traditional in practice. The charismatic leader has vision and flair, is of an extrovert and perhaps ebullient nature, can galvanise people into action as (s)he forges ahead (leaving some behind in the process!). Such a leader is often found in a pioneering situation, starting up or reviving an enterprise or political party. Two examples would be Field Marshal Montgomery and Martin Luther King.

> ***TO THINK ABOUT . . .***
> **What do you see as the positive and negative features of this style of leadership?**

Churches and church organisations have often been started or had new life put into them by charismatic personalities; William Booth's founding of the Salvation Army is an example. Such a leader often finds it difficult, however, to maintain impetus when 'his' or 'her' organisation gets past the first flush of enthusiasm and growth; it then needs consolidating into organised structures and practices and the leader needs to give some place to more accomplished organisers (note how the Billy Graham organistion has an excellent team dealing with administration).

d. Democratic (or participative)

'Being governed by the people', which is what 'democratic' means, does not imply that no leadership is needed, but that leaders, when it is practicable, enable the people in the organisation to participate in making decisions. In the secular field this is increasing; while few, if any, business firms allow the workforce to take final decisions, it is more and more recognised that consulting widely with workers before making decisions is a wise practice.

Leadership in a democratic organisation is more demanding than elsewhere because, instead of simply making decisions themselves, the leaders have to supply information to and bring out the wisdom of the rank and file, equipping them as well as possible to make sensible judgements.

This range of leadership styles from the authoritarian to the democratic can be represented by the following diagram.

RANGE OF LEADERSHIP STYLE

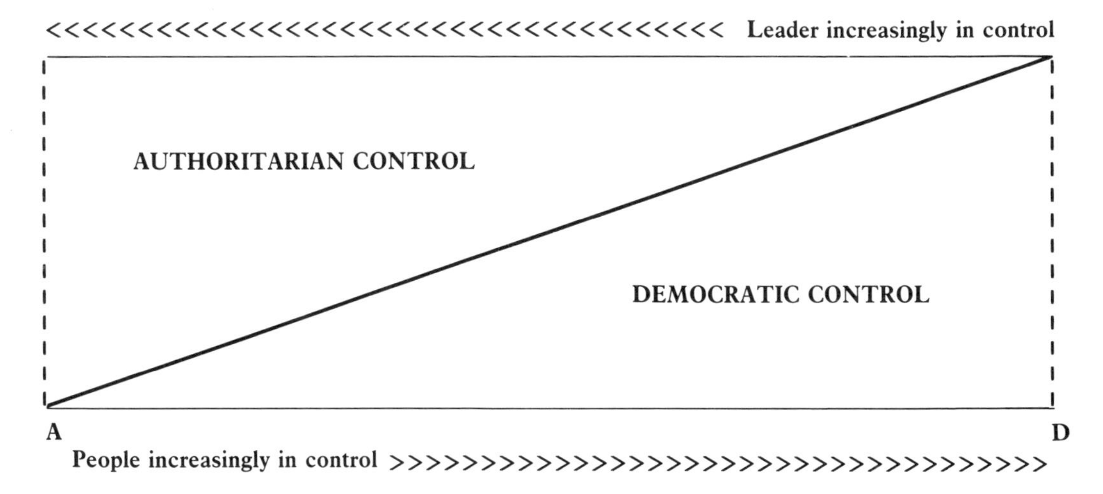

Of the four examples of leadership styles given above, the completely authoritarian style will rest under A and the completely democratic under D. The paternalistic and charismatic can be anywhere on the continuum depending on the person exercising leadership, but will usually be nearer A than D.

As we saw in Unit 3, Section C.1. Baptists believe in the 'democratic' form of government (congregational church government) for the local church. They naturally also believe that, generally speaking, 'democratic' procedures in church organisations enable us best to discern God's will and put it into effect.

This does not mean, however, that all Baptist church organisations should be equally democratically run. For instance, as we saw in Section B.1.a. above, leadership in the uniformed organisations will tend to be authoritarian rather than democratic. Primary Department children could hardly be asked to govern their affairs democratically. They will be treated mainly paternalistically, although they will usually respond better if they are asked from time to time what they want to do rather than always being ordered! Church committees and most adult organisations are democratically governed.

What has been said implies, therefore, that in a church, *as a general rule*, authoritarian government – the leaders making the decisions – is the least desirable, and 'democratic' government – the people making the decisions and discerning God's will – the most desirable, but there will be some variation.

> ***TO THINK ABOUT . . .***
> **Dwight D. Eisenhower, Supreme Commander of the Allied armies in World War II, said: 'Whenever men can be persuaded rather than ordered, when they can be made to feel that they have participated in developing a plan — they approach their task with understanding and enthusiasm'.**
>
> **Do you find anything surprising in this statement?**

2. FACTORS GOVERNING WHICH STYLE OF LEADERSHIP IS PREFERABLE

We look now at when and where leaders should vary their leadership style.

Although democratic leadership is usually preferable, there needs to be some variation. The style which is appropriate will depend on the following factors.

a. The type of organisation

We have seen that the style of leadership of a church organisation will vary according to its accepted ***structures and practices***. For example, there will be more direction of the Scouts in their activities than of the members of a church committee.

Leadership will also need to vary according to the ***people in the organisation***. If the members are professionals, executives and managers, used to giving orders, they will not take so readily to an authoritarian approach as will, say, manual workers who are more used to receiving instructions. And neither group would take kindly to patronising paternalism.

In addition, the leadership style will need to vary according to the organisation's ***present circumstances***. These can alter from time to time because of, for example, a change of personnel, the success or failure of its projects or disagreements among the members. The manager of a business or department might be a great success at one time and then, because of difficulty in adapting to changing circumstances, become less and less effective. The same can be true in a church. If, for instance, an organisation is in low water, then a charismatic approach to leadership may be called for.

b. The personality of the leader

Each of us has a leaning towards a particular style of leadership. A strong personality, with a natural leadership ability and who likes status, will find it easier to be authoritarian than will a quiet introvert who likes friendship with and support from the people being led and who, therefore, will tend to a participative style.

While you cannot completely change your personality, you can to some extent modify your approach according to the need prevailing at the time. You need to strive to be your best in any given situation.

> ***TO THINK ABOUT . . .***
> **How would you describe your own style of leadership?**
>
> **How easy or difficult do you find adapting your style to the differing contexts in which you lead and the particular aim you have at the time?**

C. *MEET EQUALLY THREE AREAS OF NEED*

1. THE TASK, THE TEAM AND THE INDIVIDUAL

A leadership team will more likely succeed in its job of leading an organisation if it both recognises that there are three areas of need to be satisfied and then does its best to meet them. These needs relate to: the TASK, the TEAM, and the INDIVIDUAL.

Dr John Adair, a leading expert in the field of management, explains this clearly and represents the relationship by the following diagram (see his *Effective Leadership*, chapter 3).

THE THREE-CIRCLES MODEL

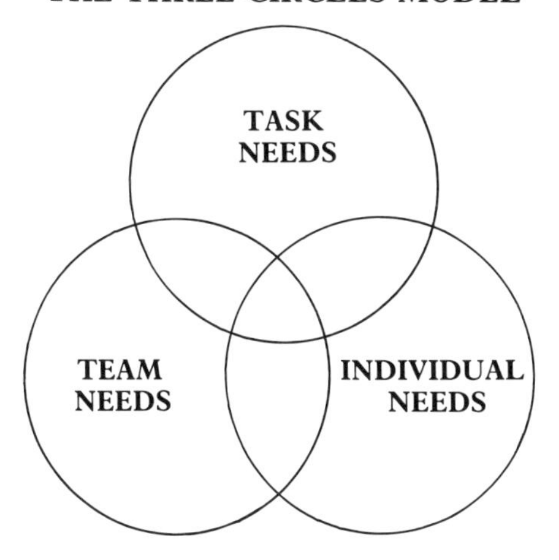

a. The need to achieve the TASK

This is an obvious need; after all that is what the team is for! Therefore, the leaders need to see clearly what are the aim and objectives of the organisation, how the task can best be done and what is each person's responsibility. They also need proper training and the necessary equipment.

b. The need to maintain TEAM cohesiveness

If the work is to be done well the leaders need to work together as a close-knit team. Eleven footballers of mediocre talent, yet welded together so as to play for the success of the team, can beat eleven of the best players who play simply for their individual glory.

So the leaders of a church organisation need bonding together by a team spirit, working for each other. This can be fostered by all members sharing in decision-making or ironing out differences of opinion, and sharing in expectation of success, social occasions, Christian fellowship and prayer.

Welded together . . . for the success of the team.

> ***TO THINK ABOUT . . .***
> **How good are you at working in a team? Do you function better when left on your own or when part of a team?**

c. The need to support the INDIVIDUAL

The corporate needs of the team should not, however, swamp the needs of each individual. All team members differ, having their own aspirations, problems, pleasures, dissatisfactions, achievements, hopes and fears. Their performance as leaders will be affected by these. Any person anxious, for instance, about employment prospects will naturally find it difficult to concentrate on the job, say, of being youth leader.

So leaders should think of each other as individuals who need help and support spiritually and in other ways. Incidentally, the more the leaders can acquire counselling skills the better they will be as leaders and as Christians generally. Two helpful primers on this subject are *Beginning Pastoral Counselling* by Ruth Fowke (Grove Booklets) and the Baptist Union Christian Training Programme manual (D6) *Pastoral Counselling* by Ron Messenger. Care for each other as individuals will strengthen not only the team members but the team as a whole which, in turn, will help achieve the task.

The diagram above illustrates, by the overlapping of the circles, this mutual dependency and interaction. Notice the circles are of equal size. Increase the size of one and, obviously, the others are smaller in comparison. Experience shows that, generally speaking, an equal concentration on the needs of the task, the team, and the individual should be maintained.

If, for instance, the leaders concentrate only on the task and forget that the team has its corporate needs and the individual members have their needs, then the task itself will not be done very well. Some businesses in the secular field have failed because they so concentrated on the task of making a profit that they forgot about people.

We in the churches should learn from this. Little success will be achieved in a church organisation if the overall leader, in his or her efforts to achieve the task, acts as a dictator and shows little interest in the team or friendliness to individuals. Nor will there be much progress in the work if the team members become so absorbed in their own enjoyment as a group that they lose sight of what they exist to do – their task. Most of us can think of church organisations or committees that so enjoy meeting together in 'fellowship' that they become introverted and contribute little to the work of the church as a whole.

By way of emphasis – the needs of the task, team and individual should, as a general rule, be met equally.

TO THINK ABOUT . . .

Write a short memo to members of a church diaconate outlining the advantages of them concentrating as equally as possible on their *task* as church leaders, the needs of the diaconate as a *team* and the needs of *individual* deacons.

Send it to your diaconate only if you think it would be helpful!

D. MOTIVATE OTHERS

One responsibility of overall leaders is to motivate to action both their fellow-leaders and the people in the organisation. We have referred to this already but now we concentrate on it.

1. MOTIVATION AND CHURCH ORGANISATIONS

While we have many things to learn from the secular business field about motivation, we must remember that leading a church organisation is different in two important respects from leading a commercial enterprise; the first difference is a disadvantage, the other an advantage.

a. The work is mainly unpaid

The majority of people who work within or for a church are volunteers, unpaid and under no contract. Leaders cannot, therefore, offer financial inducements or threat of 'the sack' as motivators. Consequently they have to work that much harder at motivating their colleagues.

b. Service is regarded primarily as a service to Christ

At least, that is how it should be. This gives leaders in a church situation a distinct advantage over leaders in any non-religious organisation.

Working hard at motivating.

That is not to deny that many in the voluntary unpaid sector of society give dedicated and sacrificial service without having a religious faith to motivate them. But it remains true that acknowledging the claims of Christ as Lord on your time and efforts is a great motivating factor. Had local churches been only secular organisations, many of them would have disappeared long ago.

> ***TO THINK ABOUT . . .***
> **How true is it that the difficulty of many churches to secure willing leaders for groups and organistions is due to a lack of consecration and commitment to Christ?**

We could cite many cases of those who have made great sacrifices because of their commitment to Christ. Paul is an outstanding example; read 2 Corinthians 11:24–28, 12:10. Other more recent examples are Gladys Aylward, Albert Schweitzer, Mother Theresa. No doubt you can think of more. It is important, therefore, to foster a commitment to Christ in yourself and in others which will lead to fruitful action within your church organisation.

2. WAYS OF MOTIVATING OTHERS

There are many ways in which church leaders can motivate others. Below are 20 examples.

a. **Foster a growing commitment to Christ, the church and the organisation.**

b. **Ensure that the organisation or committee has a worthwhile aim and clear objectives** (see Unit 3, Section B.). People will respond remarkably generously when they believe a project is worth supporting. For example, consider the amount of money and effort some congregations will devote to building a church.

c. **Help people recognise the successes which have been achieved – nothing succeeds like success.**

d. **Make activities as enjoyable as possible.**

e. **Give individuals challenging and satisfying responsibilities.**

f. **Equip them well for their task.**

g. **Show appreciation of efforts made.**

h. **Raise morale when there is disappointment.**

i. **Give continuous encouragement when a hard slog is called for.**

j. **Help people feel an integral part of a united group.**

k. **Give them other things to look forward to after the present stage is completed.**

l. **Increase their confidence in their abilities and help them grow in all areas of their lives.**

m. **Make people feel needed and wanted.**

n. **Don't give excessive attention to some and too little to others.**

o. **Set high, but not impossible, standards.**

p. **Have a pastoral concern and show in practice that you care for people.**

q. **Encourage enterprise and ingenuity.**

r. **When criticising be constructive** – let people see that you want to help them improve, and you believe they can. And usually do it in private.

s. **Include fun and humour in activities.**

t. **Be a good example 'in the field'; don't just stand on the sidelines.**

TO THINK ABOUT . . .

An elderly passenger was being thanked and congratulated by the ship's captain in front of the passengers for jumping into the sea to save a young woman. When he was invited to say a word to the admiring assembly he simply asked: 'I just want to know one thing, who pushed me'?

Funny? Yes, but reflect on who in the past has 'pushed' you into achieving what you have in life.

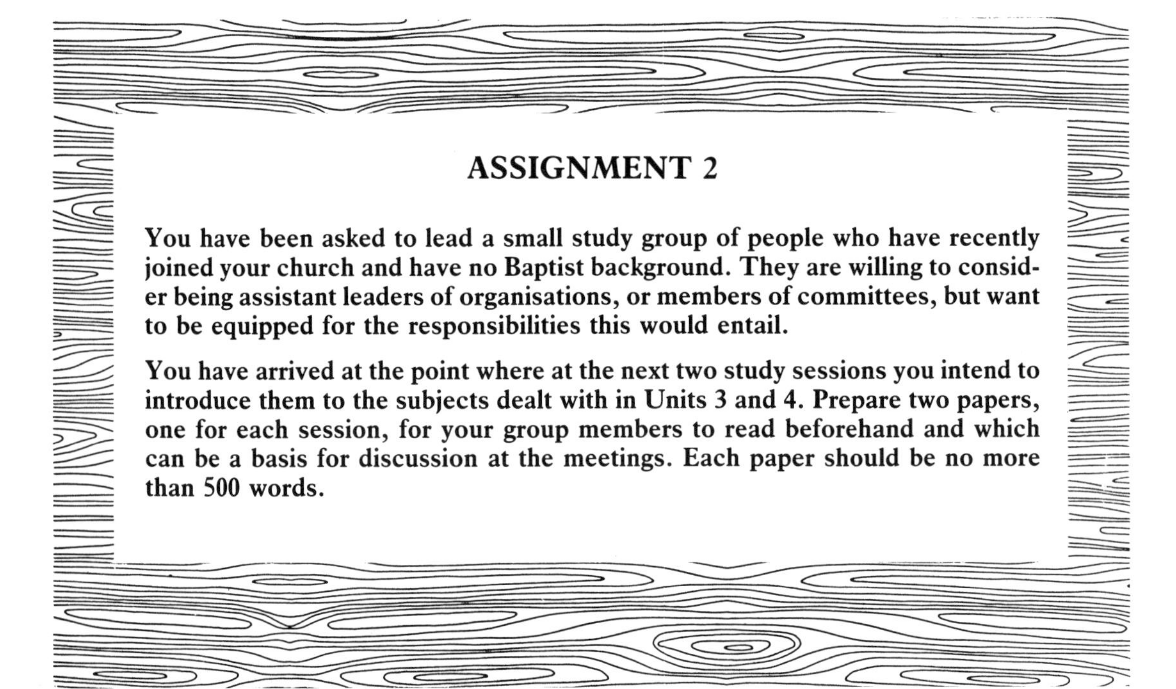

ASSIGNMENT 2

You have been asked to lead a small study group of people who have recently joined your church and have no Baptist background. They are willing to consider being assistant leaders of organisations, or members of committees, but want to be equipped for the responsibilities this would entail.

You have arrived at the point where at the next two study sessions you intend to introduce them to the subjects dealt with in Units 3 and 4. Prepare two papers, one for each session, for your group members to read beforehand and which can be a basis for discussion at the meetings. Each paper should be no more than 500 words.

UNIT 5

Good Companions – Great Colleagues

AIM: To see more clearly what is required of organisation leaders in relation to the people they work with, in order to –

A. Create beneficial relationships.
B. Manage change productively.
C. Support leadership education and training.
D. Delegate responsibilities wisely.

A. *CREATE BENEFICIAL RELATIONSHIPS*

It would be very pleasant in church life if everyone got on perfectly happily with everyone else! But, until all Christians are perfect, this will not be. Nonetheless, we should do our best to create relationships which are as harmonious as possible. Leaders should seek to spot the developing causes of ill-will in their organisations and try to remove them – prevention is better than cure. But if these do continue (and often they will!) their effects should be contained as much as possible.

We can go too far in trying to cultivate sweetness and light.

However, we can go too far in trying to cultivate all sweetness and light in relationships. There are bound to be differences of opinion and attempts to suppress the expression of these, in case strong feelings erupt, can easily cause a loss of good ideas and the useful progress they produce. Peace at any price is not a good motto. This is why the title of this section is not, 'Create *harmonious* relationships' but, '. . . *beneficial* relationships'.

> ***TO THINK ABOUT . . .***
> **How is conflict handled in your church or organisation? How could it be handled more creatively?**

If a church and its organisations are to progress, there are bound to be differences of opinion which produce tension and even conflict. This happens in the best of families, often because the members think and feel deeply. In spite of this the differences can develop clearer thinking and progressive ideas. Where family love is present, differences need not lead to divisions; in fact, they can bring people closer together.

So leaders need to remember that, while disagreements and conflict of ideas *can* create ill-will, they need not and, if handled rightly, both can be beneficial to the work of the organisation and the people themselves. We see it illustrated in the following:

- A match when struck can produce a destructive fire, or a useful light.

A destructive fire or a useful light.

- Fire under water can cause a damaging explosion, or drive a locomotive.
- A wind can damage buildings, or can sail ships, lift gliders and drive windmills.

Similarly, disagreements and conflicts of opinion need not be destructive but can be creative. They can, for example:

- Be a stimulus to finding better answers to problems.
- Clarify people's thinking.
- Produce better ideas.
- Force people to examine their motives.
- Lead to more useful actions.
- Promote the seeking and doing of God's will.

But this will require that leaders encourage people to:

- Have firm opinions, but be ready to listen to others.
- Put their point of view, but not with dogmatism.
- Speak frankly but with kindliness and sensitivity.
- Be ready of speech, but not monopolise the conversation.
- Spur people to action, but not by unfair pressurising.
- Give constructive criticism, but not demoralise.
- Question perceptively, but not by severe grilling.
- Make honest appraisal of arguments, but not score points off others.
- Be ready to accept criticism, but not develop an inferiority complex.
- Recognise problems, but accept them as challenges to be overcome.
- Enjoy fun and humour, but without hurting others.
- Make love the arbiter of what should be said and how, but not use: 'I am speaking the truth in love' as authority to wound.

TO THINK ABOUT . . .

John Adair quotes a bishop as saying: 'The sin of this diocese is niceness'. In what ways can this be true of a church? The next time you are in a committee meeting notice how:

a. you find it difficult to speak as frankly as you would like.

b. you and others, by expressing different and sometimes opposing opinions, can arrive at a better solution to a problem than if only one of the opinions was voiced.

B. MANAGE CHANGE PRODUCTIVELY

1. TYPES OF CHANGE

There are three main types of change:

a. **Unsought changes.** For example, the ceiling falls down or it starts to rain at the Sunday School picnic.

b. **Remedial changes.** They simply remedy unsought changes, such as replacing the ceiling as it was or rushing to the coaches when it rains.

c. **Creative changes.** Those that introduce new features. These can be:

i) *Expanded remedial* changes by, for instance, repairing the ceiling but at the same time making storage space above, or going to the coaches but having a quiz or sing-song with the children.

ii) *Originative* changes, such as introducing new practices, e.g. house-groups, new premises or seating arrangements.

2. THE NECESSITY FOR CHANGE

Keeping things as they are is stultifying and dangerous. William Barclay claimed that if it is true to sing, 'Change *and* decay in all around I see', it is equally true to say of living things, 'Change *or* decay . . .' Certainly the alternative to change for the better is deterioration, or death! Therefore leaders and others in an

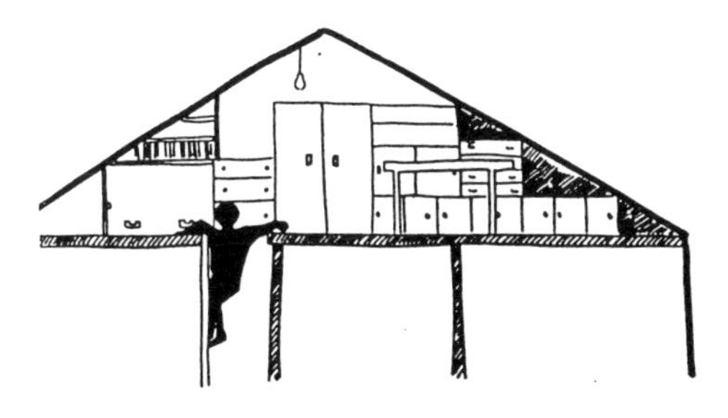

'. . . and could you get the billy-can for GB camp. It's in the box in the trunk in the cupboard behind the six stacks of old chairs!'

organisation should always be thinking ahead and putting into effect those ideas for improvement that are obviously good.

3. HOW TO INTRODUCE CHANGE

In what follows we shall consider the introduction of *creative* changes, for, if they are to be handled productively, they demand most knowledge and skill. This is easier said than done – perhaps more so in church life than elsewhere! If it is an authoritarian organisation, the leaders can introduce them without much ado, though if they are wise they will still seek the ready support of those affected. But we are assuming here that it is a 'democratic' organisation in which a change will need the majority decision of the people.

There are, of course, a lot of small changes made without any fuss and bother, though even these can cause strong hostility. Try, for example, moving a row of seats in the sanctuary! But we are thinking here of major changes, such as introducing an open youth club, forming house groups for study and pastoral care, separating the children of the Family Church from the morning service so that they do not worship with the adults, combining all the women's work under one 'umbrella', or building a Scout hut on church grounds. How best can we handle such change successfully?

a. Remember we all are basically resistant to change

Some changes we accept more readily than others – introducing some heating into a cold building will produce few objections (though the form of heating will be debated). But try replacing pews with chairs, or changing the time of the service. It is less disturbing to follow our regular customs and habits even though they are uncomfortable, and there is an in-built reluctance to change them.

b. Recognise that changes cannot be imposed against people's will

Leaders may introduce a new scheme or system, but people can then vote with their feet and not participate. Their co-operation has to be won, and this will mean providing an incentive or persuasion – usually both!

c. Choose the best person to explain what is proposed

This may not be the overall leader, or even the person who had the new idea. But it does need to be someone whom the people identify with and trust, and who is well-informed in the subject and can both explain it and answer questions clearly and sensitively.

d. Emphasise that it is *God's* will that is being sought

If the change is being proposed to non-Christians, it may not be appropriate to do this, but leaders should do so among themselves. If Christians are being asked to consider change, then the point can be made plain to them. Encourage them to pray, and give opportunities for them to do so when the proposal is under discussion.

e. Present the changes clearly

Give all the relevant information. Use visual aids if these will clarify the proposals.

f. Present it fairly

Spell out the difficulties and disadvantages of the proposed change, as well as the advantages. People should not feel that a biased presentation is being made, with some of the negative factors hidden.

If questions are given short-shrift and opposition is silenced . . .

g. Encourage questions and discussion

If questions are given short-shrift and opposition is silenced by the chairperson, the necessary majority vote may actually be obtained, but the people may be very half-hearted and there may be positive hostility from those who feel aggrieved. This may mean in practice that the proposal will not be sufficiently supported to put it into effect. An agreement may be made on Thursday to rope off the back rows of seats in the sanctuary, but may be ignored when Sunday comes round!

h. Be firm but flexible

Though change has to be introduced with care, leaders should not be diffident in advocating it. They would not bring forward proposals if they did not believe in their rightness. They should therefore present them positively and firmly and not 'chicken out' of supporting them, simply to avoid controversy. At the same time leaders should not be rigid and inflexible, but prepared to modify the proposals in light of greater wisdom, or even to drop them altogether if this seems right in light of discussion.

> ***TO THINK ABOUT . . .***
>
> **Read the following well-known prayer: 'God grant me the courage to change the things that I can change, the serenity to accept those that I cannot change, and the wisdom to know the difference'.**
>
> **Think of any occasions recently when you have needed that courage, serenity and wisdom.**

i. Be patient

Defer further discussion to another meeting if an impasse is reached, so as to give time for reflection and prayer.

j. Implement the agreed resolution positively

Too many good ideas have come to nothing simply because no one was determined and persistent enough to make them succeed. Reading some church minute books reveals how true this is.

> ***TO THINK ABOUT . . .***
> **Recall any decisions taken in some aspect of your church's life but which have not been implemented. Why has this happened?**

k. Help any continuing opposition to accept and support the change

Leaders should be seen to expect the best from opponents of the change, assuming they will recognise that, even though they did not vote for a proposition which was carried, they still should support it in practice. If treated with understanding and sensitivity, those originally hostile may, in the end, become keen supporters.

> ***TO THINK ABOUT . . .***
> **Think of one or two changes introduced recently into your church and recall the reactions for or against which they produced.**
>
> **What helpful and unhelpful steps were taken by those responsible for introducing the changes?**

C. SUPPORT LEADERSHIP TRAINING

Unfortunately, people are usually thrust into church work with no special training and often with little or no initial briefing in what is expected of them. We would not have much confidence in our doctor if he or she was simply an enthusiastic theorist. Yet we too often ask people to share in the church's work with little practical preparation beforehand or training on the job. The marvel is that they do as well as they do, but they would do better with training.

An enthusiastic theorist.

Jesus demonstrates the importance of training. He chose the twelve and trained them for their later responsibilities (e.g. Luke 8:9, 10; 11:1). And he said they must pass on his teaching to the disciples they made (Matthew 28:20). Paul maintained the practice with his converts by giving teaching in his letters and advice to his fellow leaders (see 2 Timothy 2:2).

It behoves Christian leaders, therefore, to educate and train themselves and other leaders, so that they are as well equipped as possible for the tasks to which God and the church has called them.

1. TWO NECESSARY LEARNING STAGES

a. Initial briefing

Those who appoint leaders should ensure that they are briefed before beginning their work. If this is not offered, new leaders should make sure somebody wakes up to it! Actually the written outline of what is expected should already have been supplied as a job description when a leader is asked to undertake the appointment. I was once told by a deacon that after he was elected he even had to find out for himself whether he was expected to meet in the vestry before the Sunday service and where his first deacons' meeting was to be held!

Members of committees will need to ask and read as much as possible about the field covered by their committee so as to make useful contributions. Committee leaders should see that new members get this information.

b. Continuous learning

Much is learnt, of course, from actually doing the job. But this is limited. New ideas, methods and skills can be learnt from other people who have had more experience and can give training.

> ***TO THINK ABOUT . . .***
>
> **Betty had just returned home after her first day at school: 'Well, darling,' asked her mother, 'what did they teach you?' 'Not much, Mum,' Betty answered, 'I've got to go again tomorrow'.**
>
> **Does this kind of misconception exist among Christians?**

This needs to be done, and leaders should press for it and help organise such training for themselves and others.

2. SOURCES OF KNOWLEDGE

a. Literature

There are few publications in print which concentrate solely and as comprehensively on church organisations as does this manual. But there are some with very useful material, and many on leadership in general – both Christian and secular. See Appendix B. for those that are recommended.

b. Courses, conferences, seminars

Churches can arrange their own training, possibly using specialists to provide input in whatever field they wish covered. Often, however, it is more beneficial to join in training organised on a wider basis by Baptist or other providers of courses, such as Scripture Union, Administry and Marc Europe. See Appendix B for details.

D. DELEGATE RESPONSIBILITIES WISELY

Delegation is always taking place on a casual basis. For instance, when Grace, the Women's Club leader, says to Jane, 'Will you please lock up for me tonight, I have to go early?', delegation is taking place. Obviously there is no need to organise that sort of practice in any formal way, but there comes a point when more systematic delegation becomes essential.

Strangely enough there are some leaders who will not delegate as they should. Some typical excuses are:

- 'I can't find anyone to do it', which, of course, is sometimes true, but not always. The leader must try harder.
- 'You just can't rely on people to do it properly'. Then the leader proceeds to do it badly because he or she has too much to do.

In fairness we should admit that it is at times better to do things yourself than chase around finding someone else; but the fault in church life is usually that too few people are trying to do too many things. Then, being overworked, they cannot find the time to stop and get off the tread-mill and share out the work more sensibly.

1. REASONS FOR DELEGATING

a. Allows the most strategic use of people's abilities

There is a lot of untapped ability in our churches. Have you ever had an arts and crafts exhibition in your church? If you have, you will doubtless have been surprised at the number of talents and skills which have come to light.

> ***TO THINK ABOUT . . .***
>
> **Does your church have a way of discovering the gifts of its members? If so, how effective is it? If not, what plan would you suggest that would best serve this end?**

If only we could have an exhibition of the less tangible abilities such as teaching, personal witnessing, pastoral counselling, leading worship, a gift with figures and a host of others. These often go unrecognised, sometimes by the owners themselves. Not delegating means that we are wasting the resources which God has provided, and the work of the Kingdom suffers in consequence.

b. Supplements the leaders' own abilities

No one has *all* the abilities needed for any job; there are weak points in every personality. The overall leader should make use of the other team leaders; the leadership team should bring in suitable people from outside when appropriate. If someone can and will organise the outing, chair a meeting, paint a poster, or write a report better than you, by all means let them!

c. Increases basic efficiency

In most situations if one person tries to do everything nothing will be done properly.

d. Avoids undue stress

Why is it that some previously active Christians, when they move to another church, refuse to take on any job? Often it is because they have been overworked and placed under excessive stress where they were. If only they could have delegated their responsibilities more.

> ***TO THINK ABOUT . . .***
> **List up to ten examples of delegation which have been made in your church and your organisation. In what other areas would you expect and hope to see delegation being practised?**

e. Nurtures and develops Christian personality

Because of demands made on them by Christian service, Christians become more aware of their need for extra resources. Consequently they usually seek more positively the guidance and help of God, seek to learn more about their faith, and become better developed Christians as a result.

f. Enhances the life and effectiveness of the church

If all that has been said above results from delegation, then the church and its organisations will be much better fitted to serve Christ as they should.

2. PRINCIPLES OF DELEGATING

We look now at putting delegation into practice. Ten principles are listed below. These cannot always be observed in every detail; some churches are too small to allow much delegation. But it is useful to be aware of these principles so that they can be applied where and when appropriate.

a. Have a recognised procedure for making appointments

It sometimes happens that the wrong people are in leadership positions simply because they put themselves there, or they volunteered and no one liked to refuse their offers. Maybe an unwise person invited someone to take over a job and it is now too invidious to remove them. Leaders of a church and its organisations should ensure that a recognised procedure for making appointments is agreed and then used. This will help avoid embarrassing and wrong appointments and will help make those that are best. The procedure can be worked out from the paragraphs **b.** to **j.** which follow.

'I'm just the person you're looking for.'

b. Assess the needs

There has to be some calculation of what positions need filling to facilitate the work and how many people will be needed to fill them. When a new organisation or project is set up, it means calculating from scratch. If an existing position falls vacant, the question still has to be asked: should things continue as they are, or should the position be closed or expanded?

c. Draw up a job description and terms of appointment

These should include:

- The title of the position to be held.
- The aim and objectives of the organisation/committee concerned.
- The limits of authority and to whom the appointee is responsible.
- Details of the duties to be undertaken.
- Copy of any rules/guidelines relating to the organisation/committee.
- Length of the appointment.
- Other members of the team/committee.

This is advisable for the following reasons:

- Any person considering accepting the position will be able to see in writing what it entails, reflect on it and then decide whether to accept.
- The person when appointed will be able to refer to and follow the written description.
- Later appraisal of achievement will be made easier because what has been accomplished can be measured against the expectations set out in the job description.

> *TO THINK ABOUT . . .*
> **Why may some people in Christian leadership welcome a job description and terms of appointment, whilst others may think it unnecessary?**

A sample job description is given in Appendix C.

d. Draw up job-holder's specification

From the job description a specification can be deduced of the kind of person suitable for the job. This will help those making the appointment select the right person. A sample is given in Appendix C.

e. Have an adequate system of talent-spotting

Finding the right person for a position is too often a hit-or-miss affair. We have to wonder whether God is allowed to give the guidance he wishes to. Churches do need a sensible system of identifying the abilities which reside in their church members. Careful thought needs to be given to this (see Unit 7, Section C.2, page 62).

An adequate system of talent spotting.

> *TO THINK ABOUT . . .*
> **What would you regard as an adequate and sensible system for finding people of God's choosing for leadership positions?**

f. Assess the candidate's suitability

This needs much thought, care and prayer in order that a God-directed appointment may be made. As with so much else, the selection is too often a rather haphazard exercise. When an appointment has been made –

g. Equip the person appointed for the job

This will involve the briefing and regular training mentioned in Section C above. In addition, the physical equipment necessary to run an organisation should be provided. A church should see that this is supplied and not leave it to, say, the Sunday School teachers to pay for it from their own pockets.

'Last week it was birthday cards for the children in my class — what will it be next week?'

h. Support, advise and monitor the appointee

'Delegation does not mean abdication' is the comment that applies here. Those who have made the appointment should not just leave him or her to get on with it, but should show a practical supportive interest which includes monitoring progress.

i. Trust the person appointed

At the same time, while supporting the appointed leader, those responsible should not 'breathe down his or her neck' as though the appointee cannot be trusted. Most of us are more effective when we are, within limits, self-directing.

j. Review the progress of the organisation/committee regularly

This has been described in Unit 3, Section F, page 29.

EXERCISE

Read Exodus 18: 13–27. We do not have in this passage all there is to know about delegation, but there are some important points. List, a) the reason Jethro gives for delegation and, b) the principles of delegating that he recommends to Moses. Reflect on what might have been causes in Moses himself, or his circumstances, for him not practising delegation before this?

UNIT 6

Close Encounters

AIM: To enable you to see what is required of organisation leaders in relation to the people they work with, so that they may –

A. Make the most of small groups.
B. Facilitate good decision-making.
C. Arrange and conduct devotional meetings.
D. Communicate efficiently and effectively.

A. MAKE THE MOST OF SMALL GROUPS

1. DIFFERENT TYPES OF GROUPS

The term 'group' is used to describe various collections of individuals. We can, however, divide them into two main types:

a. Informal groups

This type emerges spontaneously in all areas of life, including a church and its organisations. These groups are composed of people with like interests or aims who come together from time to time on a casual basis. In a church they may gravitate together automatically before or after a service or meeting because, for example, they come from the same part of the country, have the same occupation, have an interest in a certain sport, like the minister, don't like the minister, or are campaigning for new seating.

People with like interests or aims.

> ***TO THINK ABOUT . . .***
> **Think of your own church. On what basis do people gravitate together in informal groups?**

Informal groups are inevitable in any community. They can be useful or harmful, a mixture of both, or just neutral. They change in personnel over a period of time, or disperse entirely and other groups form. Leaders may not be very aware of exactly which groups exist, but they should realise that they can have considerable influence in an organisation. The more the leaders know about them the better they will judge how to take beneficial action in their leadership responsibilities.

b. Formal groups

In a church these are the official committees, diaconate (actually a committee), working or study groups, working parties, house groups, Sunday School teachers meetings – and so we could go on. These are deliberately and formally set up.

How big can a group be and still be called a small group? It has been discovered that a subtle, invisible, indefinable distinction occurs as you change the size of a group. Anyone working with different companies of people can discern this.

The main characteristics of a small group is that it is small enough for members to have face-to-face relationships. Obviously this would be impossible in a company of 50 or more! But, what is the maximum size? Opinions vary, but here we are thinking of a maximum of 15. Some would say that when larger than 12 most groups cease to possess small group characteristics, especially if composed of strong-minded, articulate people, and particularly if involved in decision-making (if that is so then diaconates and elderships should be limited to 12!)

Clearly there comes a point where the method of handling a group has to change as size increases. Albert J. Wollen, in *God at Work in Small Groups* claims that *dialogue* is effective with groups of seven to twelve; *question and answer*, from twelve to thirty-five; *monologue* with groups of over thirty-five.

Now, having got thus far it may be a bit tantalising to say that we have not the space in this manual to deal with this subject except in respect of decision-making in small groups. This we shall do in the next section. Those who wish to study further the subject of working with groups could start with the books mentioned in Appendix B.

> ***TO THINK ABOUT . . .***
> **To which small groups do you belong in any area of your life?**
> **What do you find attractive and helpful about these groups? What do you find unhelpful?**

B. FACILITATE GOOD DECISION-MAKING

Leaders of church organisations and committees have to meet together to make decisions about the present and future. If their aims and objectives are to be achieved, these decision-making meetings need to be efficiently run. The following advice should help.

1. BEFORE THE MEETING

a. The Secretary

The Secretary's tasks include:

- Informing and/or reminding (preferably in writing) members of the date, time and venue of the meeting.
- Arranging the agenda, often in consultation with the chairperson.
- Supplying a copy to each committee member. It is useful if a copy of the previous minutes can be supplied too.

We shall assume that the size of the meeting is no more than twelve people – i.e. a primary group. No committee should be much bigger than this, otherwise friendly relations and the necessary working-patterns cannot be established. The meeting room should, if possible, be made ready before people arrive. The seating should be arranged in a square or circle so that each person can see and speak directly to everyone else. If they can have tables in front of them for their papers so much the better. Never have them seated on both sides of a long narrow table, because control, friendly relationships and constructive participation then become very difficult.

> ***TO THINK ABOUT . . .***
> **You may have seen the television programme 'Yes, Prime Minister' or watched programmes about life at 10 Downing Street. In the light of the comments above, what suggestions would you give to the P.M. about the seating arrangements in the Cabinet Room at No. 10?**

b. The Chairperson

Sees that (s)he is well briefed on the agenda before the meeting.

2. DURING THE MEETING

a. The Chairperson

Although we are assuming that these are meetings of small groups, it may be appropriate, however, to digress for a little. Organisation leaders may well be called on at times to chair decision-making meetings of *large* groups and so we make brief comments here on what this entails.

Large decision-making meetings need to be dealt with more formally, and the customary rules of procedure and debate applied more strictly, otherwise they can get out of hand and the people become confused in making decisions. Chairpersons of such meetings should, therefore, inform themselves about the rules of procedure and debate.

Actually such knowledge will also be useful for chairing small groups, even though it will not be so strictly applied. It is easy to get into tangles at even small business meetings, often to everyone's embarrassment, and detailed knowledge of how to conduct more formal meetings helps to avoid this. See *Church Administration*, chapter 14, 'Conducting Church and Committee Meetings' (see Appendix B for details).

Returning to the small committee, let us imagine that the members are assembled and are ready to begin the meeting. The chairperson has a number of important, but hopefully not burdensome, responsibilities on his or her shoulders. These are:

i. Ensure that the people's aim is to discover God's will

This is not a group of people aiming only to discover the best human wisdom, but aiming rather that human thought and discussion shall be under the leading of the Holy Spirit. Therefore, there should be an appropriate prayer-time, a sense of Christian fellowship and a prayerful and listening attitude throughout.

ii. Seek to enable the group to make right decisions

The chairperson is not there to 'run the show', nor to do most of the talking and certainly not to impose her or his own will on the rest. The meeting should be conducted in an orderly and disciplined fashion and thus make possible God-directed decision-making. It should start on time. Regularly waiting for Mrs Smith to arrive will mean that Mrs Smith will regularly arrive late!

'I'm sorry chairman, I thought the meeting was at 7 o'clock.'

> ***TO THINK ABOUT . . .***
> **Louis XIV said: 'Punctuality is the politeness of kings'. Among Christian leaders, servants of the King of kings, why should punctuality and good time-keeping be important?**

iii. Create a friendly climate

People need to feel at home, comfortable with and supportive of each other; meeting in a home helps. Although differences of opinion may be vigorously expressed, a friendly spirit can prevail. The chairperson should try to ensure this and it helps if he or she has a friendly attitude.

iv) Be aware that hidden agendas and informal groups may exist

Hidden agendas are those matters which people seek to implement but which are not openly referred to. Some examples may help:

- A Sunday School teacher may oppose having the outing in a certain place really because of a dislike of travelling on the motorway, but doesn't like to admit it even to him or herself.
- A person may support a proposal simply because it will reduce the status of another leader.
- A youth club leader might advocate a certain closing time for the club because this would enable him to see his girlfriend earlier.
- The item 'Any Other Business' can be used by some as an opening for riding a hobby horse. It is best to take only minor matters for discussion under AOB and defer anything more important to a later agenda. The chairperson will have to decide when minor becomes major!

Members of an informal group (see Section A.1.a. above) may by prior agreement support each other along a certain line and consequently not be prepared to listen to others and modify their opinions. Thankfully, such behaviour is not so common in a church as in some other situations. The chairperson should not be unduly suspicious of these groups, but should be aware that they might exist and may be the cause of obstacles to smooth and wise decision-making.

> ***TO THINK ABOUT . . .***
>
> **When next in a committee meeting or small group, watch for the interaction between members. What 'informal groups' and 'hidden agendas' can you detect?**
>
> **What atmosphere do you sense? What communication is taking place through gestures or looks? Who do members of the group address remarks to and who do they avoid?**
>
> **Note down your observations and what you learn from them.**

v) Facilitate creative participation by all

The following are some examples of how this can be done diplomatically:

- Prompting the reticent – 'What do you say, Jack?'
- Restraining the voluble – 'Yes, that's interesting, Tom; what is your opinion, Mary?'

'Thank you Tom, but what does Mary think?'

- Controlling the aggressive – 'Thank you, Harry, we'll have to think about that.'
- Ensuring proper attention is given to the person speaking – 'Let's all hear what Jane is saying.'
- Turning conflicting opinions into stepping-stones to better decisions – 'I can see there is something in both points of view', or 'I can't see that Jim has got it right but it does help us to see Mary's point better.'
- Motivating – 'We must get a move on.'
- Initiating – 'Now, should we concentrate on . . .?'
- Information seeking – 'Does anyone know . . .?'
- Information giving – 'When this was done at . . . they . . . Does that seem sensible?'
- Opinion seeking – 'What does Tom think?'
- Opinion giving – 'It seems to me . . . how about you?'
- Clarifying – 'Yes, don't you think this is the most important factor in this matter?'
- Summarising – 'Doesn't it look as though these are the main points . . . ?'
- Piloting – 'I think we've gone off the point, let's get back to . . .'
- Encouraging – 'This seems to be well worth considering further.'

- Harmonising – 'I think you two have helped us with your different points of view to see . . . Let's move on to consider that.'

vi) Move efficiently towards decision-taking
While everyone should be given a fair opportunity to participate, do not prolong the discussion any more than is essential.

Make absolutely sure that everyone knows exactly what is being proposed. It is not essential to have it formally proposed and seconded in a small committee, though at times a formal proposition can help to make quite clear what is being decided. At times, too, it is best for the secretary to write down what is proposed and read it out before it is voted on.

Ask if all are ready to decide.

Get members to show positively whether or not they are in favour, by nods, words of mouth, or show of hands.

b. The Secretary

During the meeting:

- Reads previous minutes if not already circulated.
- Takes the minutes unless a minute secretary has been appointed. Even so, (s)he should take notes as a double-check.
- Advises the chairperson as necessary.
- Speaks to an item with the permission of the chairperson.

c. Members of committee

During the meeting they should:

- Be helpful participants in discussion and decision-making.
- Ease the task of the chairperson by supporting his/her efforts to apply the rules of procedure. Among other things this involves speaking to and through the chair, and not carrying on private conversations.

3. AFTER THE MEETING

a. The Secretary

- Writes up the minutes, or checks that they are correctly recorded.
- Takes action on decisions made.
- Ensures others take agreed action.

b. The Chairperson

- Checks (diplomatically) that decisions taken are being implemented.

C. ARRANGE AND CONDUCT DEVOTIONAL MEETINGS

These are often part of the programme of some church organisations. Advice on how to make the best of such occasions is given in Appendix A. That material is not, however, an integral part of this manual, but is included to provide practical help to any who might find it useful.

D. COMMUNICATE EFFICIENTLY AND EFFECTIVELY

1. DO WE REALLY NEED TO STUDY THIS?

You may well wonder if this is worth special study; after all, we simply have to speak or write and we have communicated. If that is what you think, just think again!

A minister writes a note to the church secretary saying, 'Please announce on Sunday that there will be Christmas singing by young people on Sunday evening December 20th.' But what exactly does it mean? Is it to happen during or after the service, in the church or around the neighbourhood? If during the service will *all* the young people sing or just a group of them? Will they do *all* the singing or will the congregation also be involved? Will the usual choir not be needed? You can probably think of some more questions which need asking.

Efficient and effective communication is a skill that needs to be learnt and learnt well, because poor communication can have unhappy, and indeed disastrous, consequences. If in doubt read Tennyson's *Charge of the Light Brigade*!

The Christian Church and the Kingdom of God have often suffered because of poor communication. Paul had to write another letter to the Thessalonians because, it seems, they had misinterpreted what was said in a previous letter about the imminence of the Second Coming of Christ. Some had actually given up working (2 Thessalonians 3:10, 11).

'Didn't anyone tell you, we can't hold the house-group here tonight?'

In church life today poor communication can mean, for example, that people go to the wrong venue for a meeting, vote at the church meeting contrary to their true opinions, send cards of sympathy to the wrong person, or be led to misjudge a person's character.

The subject of communication is an extensive and complex one. We can only consider it here in outline. If you want to study it further, the following will help:

Business Communication Made Simple by E.C. Eyre (see Appendix B.).

> ***TO THINK ABOUT . . .***
> **Re-call your own stories of poor communication leading to problems and embarrassment. What went wrong?**

2. COMMUNICATION IS FOR MOTIVATION

Leaders should communicate chiefly in order to motivate. The title of this section speaks of efficient and *effective* communication. We are speaking here not simply of passing on information which, however efficiently done, leads to no constructive action.

> ***TO THINK ABOUT . . .***
> **How does the following illustration relate to the previous paragraph? Demosthenes said to a rival orator: 'You make the audience say, "how well he speaks!". I make them say, "let us march against Philip"'!**

Paul did not write his letters mainly to pass on the latest news, nor simply to teach theology – though they did both – but to get his hearers to *do* something. For example, in Romans 12: 1, after some heavy theological argument, he continues, 'Therefore, I urge you . . . to offer yourselves . . .'

> *TO THINK ABOUT . . .*
> **Look in your Bible concordance for some more 'therefores' in Paul's Epistles. What do you learn about Paul's concern to motivate his readers?**

3. HOW TO COMMUNICATE MORE EFFICIENTLY AND EFFECTIVELY

a. Make use of all the means available

These are:

- **Spoken words**
  – Face-to-face, telephone, audio and visual tapes.
- **Written words**
  – Letters, memos, newsletters, notice-boards, etc.
- **Non-verbal language**
  – voice tone, facial expressions, gestures, body movements. Watch anyone speaking and note how even the most undemonstrative person makes use of non-verbal language to clarify or add meaning to what they are saying, e.g. a smile can soften a criticism, a wink can indicate that one is joking, a toss of the head can express scorn. Sometimes non-verbal language alone can 'speak'. For instance, notice when, during the sermon, members of the congregation fidget or have a fixed stare!

The most effective communicator uses as many of these means as possible; word of mouth is better supplemented with written information – the Sunday notices, for example.

b. Both efficient *transmission* and efficient *reception* are necessary

This is so with TV. Your receiving set may be perfect, but if the transmitter is faulty your evening's viewing is spoilt, and, of course, the same will result if the reverse is the case. So, if communication between you and others is poor you have to ask if you or the others are at fault – or both!

EXERCISE

You need a group (or groups) of three.

One member (A) makes in secret a simple model from building pieces, such as Lego. The second member (B) then listens to A describe the model and how it is put together. B then describes the model to the third member (C) who, with another set of pieces, builds the model. C is not allowed to ask questions of B, nor B of A.

Compare A's model with C's.

What lessons did you learn about the efficient transmission and reception of information?

If one or two observers are able to watch the group and comment on what takes place, all the better.

c. Both mind and emotions affect communicating

Not only the rational processes but also the feelings are involved whenever communication takes place. For example, if an overall leader feels it necessary to reprimand an assistant for some misbehaviour, the leader will have some anxiety about how best to go about it and what reactions might result. The leader's manner will betray this. As soon as the assistant realises what the conversation is about, emotions of embarrassment, guilt, anger, or sense of injustice will be aroused in him/her also.

Such emotions will cloud the perceptions of them both. What they *think* they hear will probably not be exactly what was *said*, so that the account each of them gives afterwards of the conversation will differ one from the other. Their accounts will be different again from the report of a detached observer.

d. Help people to hear what is actually said

You may say, 'Well that's obvious!', and so it is, but it demands skill to do it properly. The trouble is that, however clear may be the speaker's diction and however good is the listener's hearing, there are often factors which distract attention. It may be the appearance or habits of the speaker, something on the listener's mind – a problem or a pleasure –, a lack of interest in the subject, concern about what to say in response, emotional factors (see c. above), or there may be activity and noise in the background.

So, while the speaker must enunciate words as clearly as possible, there is also the need to counteract any distractions suffered by the listener. The following are some suggestions:

- Limit surrounding distractions as much as possible; better still find a more suitable location.
- Ensure the conversation is face to face.
- Avoid habits and movements which reduce the listener's concentration.
- Express yourself arrestingly and attractively.
- Help the listener to see that the subject is relevant.

Avoid habits and movements which reduce the listener's concentration.

- Be ready openly to admit the presence of emotional factors if such exist – this will help reduce the inner stress of both.

e. Help people to understand what is meant

> ***TO THINK ABOUT . . .***
> **Reflect on this much used quotation: 'I know that you believe you understand what you think I said, but I am not sure you realise that what you heard is not what I meant'.**

Simply hearing what is said is not enough.

Therefore:

i. Say and write what you actually mean
You know what you mean, but your words and sentences may not truly express it. You might say, 'They only are having sandwiches', when what you meant was, 'They are having only sandwiches.' Or, 'What are you looking there for?', when what you meant was, 'Why are you looking there?'

ii. Carefully watch the listener and note reactions and responses

These will give you some indication whether (s)he is comprehending what you are saying.

iii. Guard against and correct the misinterpretations listeners can put on what is said.

For various reasons people can easily put wrong constructions on what they hear. For example, someone asked me how a person was who had just had an operation.

'Oh, he is back in the ward and has come through the operation all right.'
'So we can say *the operation has been a success* can we?'
'No, we don't know yet whether it has been successful or not, just that he has come through it and is back in the ward.'

The italics show where the incorrect construction was put on what I said. Did I lay myself open to be misunderstood? How could I have expressed it in the first place to guard against this?

> *TO THINK ABOUT . . .*
> **How would you put it?**

For various reasons people also draw the wrong inferences from what is said. Here are some:

- They *expect* to hear something different from what is actually said. During the Sunday notices, for example, they may think they hear a particular date of a meeting because they thought that was when it would be – and turn up on the wrong day!
- The emotional factors mentioned above cloud or distort the thought processes. 'You look lovely tonight', says Dick to Joan as a casual comment, not knowing that she has a crush on him. Joan takes it seriously and walks home on air, but later comes sadly down to earth.
- People may not relish what they hear and the subconscious mind then blanks it out or changes it to something more pleasant. Is this why the disciples did not accept that Jesus was to be put to death, even though he said it so plainly on a number of occasions (e.g. Luke 18:31–34)?

Leaders need to make allowance for these and other obstacles when they are communicating.

iv. Give the listeners opportunity to ask for clarification.

v. Repeat complex ideas, using different words or images.

f. Conversation means not only speaking but listening

In a conversation it is rare that one person does all the talking. If (s)he does, (s)he shouldn't! So leaders should apply all that has been said in this section to themselves as listeners. Listening well is an essential factor in all areas of leadership as a whole and, not least, in the art of communication.

Children, especially, deserve to be listened to by leaders.

> *TO THINK ABOUT . . .*
> **In the next few conversations you have, note carefully how often someone interrupts what you are saying and how often you interrupt (or are tempted!) another speaker.**
>
> **What do you learn from this? How do you feel when you are interrupted?**

ASSIGNMENT 3

You have recently agreed to become Sunday School Superintendent (or whatever the title is in your church). You soon have to chair a teachers' meeting for the first time. On the agenda, amongst other items, will be:

1. **Arranging the next Sunday School summer outing.**
2. **Finding a replacement for the present leader of the Primary Department who is leaving the district in a month's time.**
3. **Resolving the problem of finding a larger room for the Beginners Department which is rapidly expanding. The teachers are getting restive because of the difficulties this creates. The Adventurers (young teenage group) – which is decreasing in numbers – occupy the most suitable room but they much prefer that because, among other things, they can more easily use their overhead projector there.**
4. **The previous Superintendent upset Mrs A, one of the teachers, because he would not allow her 13 year old daughter – who has made no Christian profession – to teach in the Beginners Department. You hear on the 'grapevine' that she intends to raise the matter under Any Other Business.**

Write a memo for your own private guidance on how best to handle the meeting (a) generally, and (b) in respect of these particular items. Bear in mind what you have learnt during this course so far. (1000 words should be ample.)

UNIT 7

What Good Leaders are Made Of

AIM: To provide a description of:

(a) the personal endowments, i.e. the desirable characteristics and particular abilities, appropriate in those who lead church organisations;

(b) the factors to be taken into account by those responsible for appointing the most suitable leaders to church organisations/committees.

Areas covered:

A. Desirable characteristics. B. Particular abilities C. Choosing the leaders.

INTRODUCTION

God does not intend everyone to be a leader of a church organisation or member of a committee. It is true, of course, that God has *work* for everyone. But he does not expect everyone to undertake every kind of task. He has given each person only certain capabilities. Therefore, only a proportion are meant to be leaders. Paul makes this plain in his letter to the Romans – ' . . . in one body we have many members, and all the members do not have the same function' (12:4).

This means that those appointing leaders of church organisations have to identify the most suitable candidates. What should they look for – what personal endowments best equip people to be Christian leaders? These fall into two main groups, which we will call:

A. Desirable characteristics.
B. Particular abilities.

Just wait till they look at me!

Before going further we must recognise that no one has *all* the suitable personal endowments for leadership, and none of them in full measure. God has to use defective instruments, or, to take Paul's metaphor of the body, the limbs of Christ's body are all to some degree disabled.

We see this illustrated in the early church. For instance, even Paul and Peter had a stand-up argument because Peter had reneged on his previous conviction that the Gospel was for Gentiles as well as Jews (Galatians 2:11–16). Then John Mark, on their first missionary journey, deserted Paul and Barnabas; unfortunately this led to a row between the two leaders and they split up (Acts 15: 36–4).

So, we cannot expect to find any faultless leaders. Nevertheless it is good to see what the ideal is and aim for it for ourselves and for others. First, let us ask what are the desirable characteristics for all Christian leaders.

> ***TO THINK ABOUT . . .***
> **Before reading on, what eight characteristics would you regard as most desirable for Christian leaders and why?**

A. DESIRABLE CHARACTERISTICS

These are of two types:

1. Spiritual and moral qualities.
2. Personality traits.

1. SPIRITUAL AND MORAL QUALITIES

There is no definitive list of these qualities and any that is drawn up will not satisfy everyone, but the following will probably be acceptable to most people.

- **Faith in God.**
- **Dedication to Christ** – acknowledging him as Lord.
- **Spirituality** – inner experience of Christ.
- **Love for others** – not just feelings, but active pastoral concern.
- **Firm convictions** – having clearly identified beliefs.
- **Commitment to the task** – taking it as a call of God and putting one's heart into it.
- **Humility** – including having a servant attitude.
- **Integrity** – honesty, sincerity, trustworthiness.
- **Consistency** – not 'blowing with the wind'.
- **Industry** – steady application to the task.
- **Disciplined behaviour** – following the right and shunning the wrong.
- **Reliability** – dependable at all times.
- **Persistence** – persevering in pursuing the right and the good.
- **Moral courage** – acting according to your conscience in spite of opposition.
- **Patience** – with difficult people and circumstances.

> ***TO THINK ABOUT . . .***
> **Identify from the above list and your own list what you think are your four strongest qualities and your four weakest. If you think you can stand it, get a close friend to identify your qualities in a similar way. Only do so if you can bear the honesty and remain friends!**

These qualities are of prime importance for Christian leaders because:

- They open the door to God and his glory in the life and affairs of the church.
- They enable God's will to be better discerned.
- They ensure that leaders act under the enabling of the Holy Spirit.
- They help leaders to be good examples to those they lead.

That, no doubt, is why Paul concentrates mainly on spiritual and moral qualities when giving advice to Timothy and Titus on the appointment of elders and deacons (1 Timothy 3:1–13; 5:17; Titus 1:5–9), and why it is these that were stressed when 'the Seven' were appointed (Acts 6:1–3). Those making appointments must resolve to ensure that those appointed have the highest possible standard of spiritual and moral qualities.

Once again we must stress that no perfect person will be found, and the standard of qualities available will vary from church to church, depending on the situation of each. A lower standard may have to be accepted, for instance, in a church where there are not many potential leaders to choose from. The standard may also vary from organisation to organisation. It is crucial to have a higher standard of qualities in some organisations than in others – the young people's group, for instance, requires leaders equipped to give a more positive spiritual input than, say, the mothers and toddlers group.

> ***TO THINK ABOUT . . .***
> **Is this last sentence fair comment? Why do you answer as you do?**

It is interesting that Paul tells Timothy not to appoint recent converts as bishops at Ephesus (1 Timothy 3:6), but Titus was given no such instruction. Timothy was told to appoint deacons as well as bishops (1 Timothy 3:8), Titus was given no such instruction (Titus 1:5). Was this because there were fewer leaders available for Titus at Crete?

But although there will be variation in the standard of spiritual and moral qualities required in different situations, there needs to be a *minimum spiritual* standard below which a church will not appoint someone to leadership. What should that minimum be? Each church must decide for itself!

> ***TO THINK ABOUT . . .***
> **What would you consider the minimum requirement?**

Some would say *all* leaders – the overall leader and the assistants – should be committed Christians and church members. How can you ensure, they would argue, the aim of the church is pursued if leaders do not fully share that aim?

Others would agree that is the ideal minimum but that under some circumstances, particularly where there is shortage of personnel, it may be advisable to permit the appointment of *assistant* leaders who are not church members or, under some circumstances, not Christians, so long as the overall leader is at least a Christian, and preferably a church member. For instance, they might say that Sunday School *helpers* who are not professing Christians may be used in a Primary Department.

Yet others may agree that the ideal minimum is that all leaders should be Christians and church members but that at times it may be wise to use a non-Christian as even the *overall* leader. For instance, they might argue that the church-sponsored Scout Troop could find itself in the situation where it would have to close down if the church will not accept the only leader available because he is not a Christian. They would say that to accept him would be better than to lose contact with the boys who would otherwise receive no Christian influence from a church. Those who take this point of view might say that this should be permitted only as a rare exception when special circumstances require it.

> ***TO THINK ABOUT . . .***
> **Reflect back over these last three paragraphs. What position do you take on these issues? What leads you to respond in that way?**

2. PERSONALITY TRAITS

We have been considering spiritual and moral qualities for leaders which really all Christians should seek to develop. But more than these are required of suitable *leaders* in a church. There are many dedicated Christians in our churches who are outstanding both spiritually and morally but are not suited to leadership. No doubt you can think of some quiet, humble believers who exemplify Christlikeness as few others do, but who would never fit into a leadership role – and they would be the first to say so.

Although the Pastoral Epistles do not pretend to give a comprehensive list of the requirements of elders and deacons, it must be of importance that they do include characteristics which are not specifically spiritual or moral (1 Timothy 3: 2–13; Titus 1:5–9). For example, good sense, peaceableness, hospitality, capacity for teaching, ability to manage a household, are all mentioned.

We need to ask ourselves what other characteristics are necessary for leadership besides the qualities we have just been considering. This brings us to those desirable characteristics we have called, *personality traits.*

Everyone of us has certain features within our personal make-up which determine how well we perform at any occupation. For instance, a concert pianist will perform better for having a reasonable amount of self-confidence, so will a preacher; a pastoral counsellor will be more helpful for having an evident degree of sensitivity and wise judgement; a leader will be more effective if (s)he has vision, and is venturesome and decisive. These often are inborn traits. On the other hand, they may be acquired through experience and they can be enhanced through training.

> *TO THINK ABOUT . . .*
> **Do you consider you tend towards a high or low self confidence? How is your performance as a leader affected by your level of self confidence?**

What are the traits which help to make for good leadership? There is no clearly defined and universally accepted list. People differ to some extent in what they would include and the importance they would attach to each one. But the following would probably find a place in the list of most.

> *TO THINK ABOUT . . .*
> **Before moving on, what six words would you choose to sum up your own personality traits. If working through this material with others, what would they say were the chief features of your personality?**

- **Vision** – having high ambitions and aims for the Kingdom, and seeing what is needed to achieve them.
- **Readiness to learn** – there is a lot to be learnt about leadership, not least from your mistakes.
- **Wise judgement** – this is necessary because vision and knowledge are not enough, they still have to be wisely used.
- **Decisiveness** – making up your mind without dithering.
- **Adventurous spirit** – taking creative and courageous initiatives.
- **Natural leadership ability** – having drive and enthusiasm, and the charisma to get people to follow.
- **Self-confidence** – knowing what you can do and acting accordingly without hesitation.

Learn from your mistakes.
When you come a cropper — don't give up, get up and carry on a wiser person

- **Ability to relate easily** – able to get on with (most!) people.
- **Sensitivity** – able to enter into people's feelings (which includes readiness to listen) and respond appropriately.
- **Flexibility** – readiness to change and adapt as necessary.
- **Firmness** – though sensitive, being able to take a strong line and withstand pressures. Tender yet tough.
- **Organising and administrative ability** – speaks for itself.
- **Sense of humour** – if you need it explained, you haven't got it!
- **Ability to judge between the ideal and the possible** – having high aims and ambitions, but not going off on wild goose chases.
- **Efficiency** – a lot of plans founder because people do not carry them through with attention to detail.
- **Facility in communicating** – able to express yourself clearly and persuasively.

> ***TO THINK ABOUT . . .***
> **Award yourself marks 0–10 according to how much of each of the above traits you think you possess. Don't be too demoralised by the result! If you are really brave — or foolish — get someone who knows you well to do the same for you. But do not be upset by the result, or fall out over it.**

Everyone should recognise, of course, that no one person will have all the personality traits we have been describing, and none to the highest degree. You might be a natural leader, but not good at administration; able to communicate well but not very decisive; efficient but not very wise in judgement. This fact makes team leadership such an advantage because one person can make up for what another lacks. Nevertheless the best available should be sought.

B. PARTICULAR ABILITIES

1. ROUND PEGS IN ROUND HOLES

We have been looking at those personal endowments which we have called *desirable characteristics* and which, ideally, all Christian leaders should possess, whatever their position of leadership. Now we come to what we call *particular abilities*. These relate to competence in doing a particular job. No one person can be expected to be so versatile as to have them all. For instance, the choir leader may not be suited to run the creche; a Sunday School teacher may not be fitted to be a deacon; or the catering convener to be a scoutmaster. It is a case of finding and appointing those best suited to each situation.

'A little more pianissimo please on the sustained crying on upper 'C' sharp.'

C. CHOOSING THE LEADERS

1. DRAW UP JOB-HOLDERS' SPECIFICATIONS

First a church has to decide what *kind* of people will best fit into the positions of leadership which need filling. To do this, job-holders' specifications need to be drawn up (see Unit 5, section D.2.d., page 46 and Appendix C).

2. DISCOVER POTENTIAL LEADERS

Certain abilities are needed to lead in each particular organisation or committee. Therefore, those making appointments to each position need to discover in whom the appropriate abilities are located. In a very small church most of these abilities are obvious, although even there they can be surprisingly hidden. In a larger church, however, they have to be searched for by a carefully worked out system. Any system will need to vary from church to church, but the following suggestions should provide some ideas.

Follow the guidelines for making staff appointments provided within the church's written rules.

Publicise the vacancies – existing, or anticipated – by the various information agencies within the church. For example, try a 'Job Centre' poster on the notice board, or an item in the weekly 'bulletin' or church magazine. Problems can arise if unsuitable people apply; therefore the advertisements should be so worded that it is obvious that only *inquiries* are asked for and not firm applications, and that offers may not be taken up.

But more than this will be needed! Such publicity often meets with little response. Church leaders will need to give thought to other ways of discovering potential leaders. These may include discussion among themselves and with the present staff of the organisation, and individual inquiries. If an 'Offers and Requests Canvass' has taken place (as described in Appendix C), then hopefully there will be a list of people who have offered their services and who can be considered. If appropriate, the Hidden Abilities Questionnaire can be used (see the Group Training Course, Period 7, page 90).

As new people settle into the congregation they can be invited at an appropriate time to complete a questionnaire asking what gifts they have to offer. To help their understanding of the church and its needs, it would be very useful to have a Church Handbook which they could be given (see Appendix C for suggestions about content).

> ***TO THINK ABOUT . . .***
>
> **Some argue that the main leadership of a church should discover and identify members' God-given gifts, then see that structures and opportunities are created to deploy those gifts.**
>
> **Others argue that the structures or organisations best suited to the church's life and mission need to be created first, then suitable leaders sought.**
>
> **Is one position right and the other wrong?**

3. DECIDE ON THE MOST SUITABLE CANDIDATE

In spite of every effort it is unlikely that a person with *all* the desirable abilities will be found for a particular position; it is rather a case of finding the best available. In a small church the temptation can be to ask people to take on tasks for which they are totally unsuited. Better make no appointment, or a temporary one, than have the wrong person in position. It can also be that the few are being overworked. It is wiser to undertake a few essential things rather than attempt too much. In larger churches more abilities are available – it is a matter of discovering them.

> ***TO THINK ABOUT . . .***
>
> **'Better make no appointment . . . than have the wrong person in position'.**
>
> **Is that wise and realistic counsel for a small church, or is it a counsel of perfection not always workable in a rural or inner city church?**

Now comes the task of assessing the suitability of the person or persons available. In business life there are formal references and interviews and, where appropriate, test exercises. In a church, however, we know that, except for paid appointments, all such formalities are not readily acceptable. Nevertheless, as much care as possible should be taken. Too often unwise appointments are made which damage the work and witness of a church.

And much care *can* be taken in making appointments. Informal inquiries and soundings can be made of people who know the candidates. Forthcoming vacancies can often be anticipated months ahead and thought given immediately to, and inquiries made about, possible appointees. Sometimes, potential candidates can be given responsibilities in positions similar to those which will become vacant, so that their abilities can be evaluated. If this is done it should be done informally and without any commitment on either side.

TO THINK ABOUT . . .
To what extent should good leaders be responsible for training and encouraging potential successors?

When the appointment is about to be made, the candidates should be talked and prayed with, perhaps not in a formal interview, so that they can frankly discuss the task and how they feel about their capabilities. Sharing details of the job description with them will be helpful.

So if sufficient forethought is given, there are various ways in which assessments of people can be made. For the sake of the church, the Kingdom and the people concerned, it needs to be done.

TO THINK ABOUT . . .
Remember, assessment is not easy! When Viscount Montgomery was an officer cadet at Sandhurst, his company commander called him in one day and said, 'Montgomery, I have been watching you very carefully and you will never rise above the rank of Major'. 'Well', said the Field Marshal in a talk to a later generation of cadets at Sandhurst, 'he was wrong. It was he who never rose above the rank of Major'!

EXERCISE

You are soon to retire from being the overall leader of the Women's/Men's Fellowship (choose which you wish!) and you have been asked by the deacons to recommend to them a procedure for appointing your successor.

Draw up the paragraph on the *job-holder's specification* which you would include in the document you submit to the deacons.

UNIT 8

Preparing and Supporting Leaders

AIM: To show you what church organisation leaders need from their church to ensure they are well equipped for their tasks.

Areas covered:

A. Before leadership is contemplated.
B. When invited to take the position.
C. When taking the position.
D. When in position.

We have noted before that people are too often expected to take on jobs in their church with little preparation, training and practical support. But church work is Christ's work and Christ's work deserves the best. To get the best from church leaders the following is necessary.

A. BEFORE LEADERSHIP IS CONTEMPLATED

Preparation for Christian service needs to be provided by *each* church for *every* Christian. All potential future leaders will benefit from this. How should Christians obtain it? By –

1. OBSERVING WHAT HAPPENS IN PRACTICE

Most church members get some idea of what Christian service entails in the different areas of church life by seeing people actually doing it. They learn something of what being a deacon involves, for instance, by seeing the deacons emerge from the vestry just before worship on Sundays, serve at the Communion table, perhaps welcome people at the door, and occasionally speak at Church Members' Meetings. From that comes a picture of what being a deacon involves. The same applies to other jobs in the church.

This is all assuming that what is observed is good practice and not bad. Observing a leader

tearing around, trying to prepare a room for a meeting at the last minute, is not very helpful for the potential colleague or successor.

However, observation does provide a useful education. But it is not enough. For one thing, a lot of what the different jobs involve is not seen by the ordinary church members. The deacons are not seen at work in deacons' meetings, which is perhaps their most demanding task. Sunday School teachers may be seen shepherding their children out of church on Sunday mornings, but not seen actually teaching.

Furthermore, observation by itself is not enough. The theological and administrative principles which govern (or should govern) what is done in church, and how it should be done, also need to be known. For example, what principles tell us that we should have deacons, and what their role, responsibilities and authority should be in Baptist churches? What principles lie behind the way they carry out their functions? Why have Sunday Schools (or whatever they may be called)? What should teachers actually be trying to do; what, in other words, should be the aim and objectives of the Sunday School? Why adopt the methods used? The church leaders – and members – should know the answers.

There is much then for potential leaders to learn, apart from what they see happening in church. How can they learn these things?

> ***TO THINK ABOUT . . .***
> **What principles do you think undergird Baptist churches having a concern for work with and among children and young people?**

2. HEARING FROM THE 'FIELD-WORKERS'

To make this possible, those involved in the different areas of church work can be invited to tell their story and share their successes and their problems with the church members. It can be done in more attractive ways than straight reporting. Illustrative material can be used; situations can be dramatised. What about the mothers and toddlers group doing a role play? Or the Scouts a mock camp? Or the catering committee a sample committee meeting? The Church Members Meeting can forego some of the secondary items on which it spends too much time to make room for these!

> ***TO THINK ABOUT . . .***
> **How does or could your church's members' meetings give opportunity for different aspects of the church's life being presented and cared for?**

3. RECEIVING SYSTEMATIC TEACHING

Christians should be helped to recognise that the Christian life means service (not only in church, of course, but this is the subject for this course). To that end they need systematic teaching, via the minister and in other ways, on the fundamental principles which we noted in Section A.1. above. Here are some of the principles which should be dealt with.

a. Ministry is by the whole church

If the church is to act as the body of Christ, *all* Christians, as members of that body, should be involved in Christian service (Ephesians 4: 11, 12, New English Bible and Good News Bible).

b. Differences of abilities

As Paul makes plain to the Romans, none of us has all gifts (Romans 12: 4–8). We are equipped for particular kinds of service, not for them all. This means that we need:

i) Help to discern what our abilities are.
ii) Opportunity, so far as possible, to exercise them.

c. Biblical principles of leadership

It is crucial that potential leaders in a church are educated in these principles (see Unit 2, page 14). Only then shall we adequately secure the right leaders, with the right motives, properly motivated and enabled to fulfil their role effectively.

TO THINK ABOUT . . .
Why did Jesus spend nearly three years teaching his disciples instead of sending them 'into all the world' straightaway?

B. WHEN INVITED TO TAKE THE POSITION

Those invited to become leaders or members of committees will need access to certain information before saying, yes.

1. THERE IS NEED FOR SUCH A LEADER

It does not follow that because the post to which you are invited has existed in the past it is necessary for the present and future. Often the tendency is for practices to continue under their own momentum without question. Have the church leaders inquired properly whether or not this should remain? If it is a new post, has proper thought and prayer been given to it before setting it up? You need to know.

2. A SATISFACTORY APPOINTMENTS PROCEDURE HAS BEEN FOLLOWED

Has the group responsible for making the appointment been constructively involved, or has perhaps just one person taken action? Have proper efforts been made to find the most suitable candidate? Anyone invited to a post needs to feel that this is not only a call of the church but of God himself and, therefore, needs to know that adequate thought and prayer have been given to the matter.

> *TO THINK ABOUT . . .*
> **From your own experience or the experience of others, what have you learned about the various ways in which a call from God can come?**

3. A DESCRIPTION OF THE AIM AND OBJECTIVES OF THE ORGANISATION/COMMITTEE

Leaders obviously need to know these in order to put their hearts into the jobs (see Unit 3, section B., page 24).

4. A JOB DESCRIPTION AND TERMS OF APPOINTMENT

No one should accept an appointment without knowing what it entails (see Unit 5, Section D.2.c., page 46).

5. A COPY OF CHURCH RULES (IF ANY)

6. A COPY OF THE ORGANISATION'S RULES/GUIDELINES

7. OPPORTUNITY FOR CONFERENCE AND PRAYER WITH THOSE MAKING THE APPOINTMENT

To satisfy yourself that the invitation is a thoroughly thought-out call of the church and of God, you need to talk and pray with those responsible for making it.

> *TO THINK ABOUT . . .*
> **How does the following relate to Section B above?: 'Too many decisions are made on the basis of too little information.'**

C. *WHEN TAKING THE POSITION*

Assuming that you have now agreed to become a leader of a church organisation or member of a committee, what do you need?

> *TO THINK ABOUT . . .*
> **Have the three points noted here been illustrated in your experience as a Christian leader?**

1. A FORMAL PUBLIC APPOINTMENT

It is a pity when people are allowed just to drift into a position as though it was of little significance. Some kind of official recognition is appropriate and useful because it:

- Gives the leaders a due sense of responsibility – it is made plain that people are relying on them.
- Elicits the respect that makes leadership easier.
- Produces in others greater readiness to support the leaders practically and, not least, in prayer.

This can be done in a variety of ways. Deacons are often inducted at a Communion service. Church organisation leaders can be introduced to a Sunday congregation and then prayer offered. Even an inexperienced, temporary Sunday School teacher should at least be formally introduced to the class or department where (s)he will work and then be welcomed with prayer.

2. BRIEFING ON IMMEDIATE ACTION

This is dealt with in Unit 5, Section C.1.a., page 43.

3. WELCOME BY FELLOW-WORKERS

New members of a leadership team or committee can feel isolated, uncertain and even, at times, unwanted. The best efforts will be obtained from them if they feel wanted, they are in the company of friends, and their contribution is valued.

> ***TO THINK ABOUT . . .***
> **Note how Paul's commissioning by the leaders in the Jerusalem church (Galatians 2: 7–10) corresponds to what is advocated in this Section C.**

D. WHEN IN POSITION

1. CONTINUING SUPPORT FROM FELLOW-WORKERS AND CHURCH MEMBERS

Initially there may be fulsome promises of support which are not kept as time goes on. But organisation leaders and committee members can get very low at times, because little or no progress is being made in the work or because others criticise, problems seem intractable or relationships are strained. Stress can be a very debilitating factor even in (or especially in?) Christian work.

If a leader is to be continually motivated, and receive the inner resources he or she needs, the church as a whole and fellow-workers in the organisation or committee should be concerned continually to provide appropriate spiritual, moral and practical support. This should not be left to chance but should be planned for and properly organised by the church. This support should express itself in prayer and verbal encouragement, but also in tangible support. The following are therefore important.

2. STRUCTURES AND PRACTICES THAT FACILITATE THE WORK

If it is necessary, as we have claimed in Unit 3, section C., that leaders should work within the structures and practices of their church, it is equally necessary that those structures and practices should make it as easy as possible for leaders to do their work. There should be:

- Easy access to those 'higher up' in the organisation. For example, do you have to chase after an elusive church secretary, who appears constantly overworked?
- A well-administered system for dealing with pleas for advice and assistance. Are these dealt with speedily and constructively by the church leaders and church meeting?
- A good communication system within the church. For instance, how easy is it to get notices publicised in the weekly bulletin or church magazine. Do the Sunday School teachers, through leaving early, miss some important notices made in the morning service? How well is the church magazine used for publicity purposes?
- An efficient method of booking rooms. It is important to avoid the frustrations and squabbles which easily arise over this.

3. NECESSARY FINANCIAL, MATERIAL AND PERSONNEL RESOURCES

Organisations often work on a shoe-string budget with the leaders themselves subsidising their work out of their own pockets. If the church members believe that organisations should exist, they should support them adequately.

Second-rate, out-of-date or non-existent equipment is too often unnecessarily tolerated. Only the best and most efficient should be good enough for Christ's service.

Too often, a few leaders are left to struggle on in their work with a shortage of helpers when the church should be making more imaginative and resolute efforts to discover and utilise the unharnessed abilities which may exist (see Unit 7, section C.2. p.62).

Spot the non-deliberate mistakes!

> ***TO THINK ABOUT . . .***
> **Identify the positive ways in which your church provides both continuing support for leaders and structures which help the work.**
>
> **What further steps could be taken to improve such support?**

4. REGULAR EDUCATION AND TRAINING

This has been covered in Unit 5, section C. p.43.

5. REGULAR REVIEW OF PROGRESS

The need and methods for reviewing an *organisation* are described in Unit 3, section F. Reviewing the performance of an *individual* however, is a matter which, if not handled wisely, can demoralise and create ill-will. This danger is greatly reduced by looking not at the past performance but setting targets for achievement in the future. This can be done by the technique, already referred to, of Management by Objectives (MBO). The technique makes review and appraisal easier in that objectives are first set for an organisation or individual. Then, after a set period, a check is made as to how well the objectives have been met. This proves to be a stimulus to progress.

It can also be useful to engage in a *self-appraisal* exercise. A sample questionnaire for an assistant youth club leader is given in Appendix C. Questionnaires relevant to other leadership positions can be drawn up by people well-acquainted with the abilities required.

TO THINK ABOUT . . .

What relevance has the following saying to what is said in Section D above. 'The world is full of willing people — some willing to work, the rest willing to let them'!

ASSIGNMENT 4

1. **Repeat Exercise 1, (Unit 1, page 11) using the text below. Now note for your own interest how what you have learnt on the course is reflected in your present judgement of the faults or deficiencies in this imaginary case, compared with your earlier judgement.**
2. **Having done that, describe what the minister, deacons, church members' meeting and youth club leader and assistant leaders should do to remedy the defects and avoid them in the future. Maximum 1000 words.**

The minister of a church sees in his Sunday congregation a young fellow whom he recognises as having attended for a few weeks. 'We ought to try and use him in the church somehow,' he says to himself during the offertory. 'How can we do it?' he wonders.[1] 'Perhaps the youth club could do with an assistant leader. I'll ask him afterwards. He may even join the church as a result.'

So, after the service he approached the young man and asked if he would be assistant youth club leader. 'Yes, if you like,' was the reply. 'When should I start?' 'Oh, go along tomorrow night at seven and tell them I've sent you. What's your name, by the way?' 'Don', he was told.

Don went home to his wife who had been looking after the children and told her that he was going to help at the church youth club.

Along he went on Monday night at 7pm. He found that things were not quite as he had imagined. A crowd of teenage boys were larking about around the locked door of the church hall; but there was no leader or staff. This, they said, was usual.

After ten minutes the leader and a helper did appear. 'What are you doing here?' Don was abruptly asked. When he explained, he received a frosty mumbled response. By now the youngsters were running riot in the hall, whereupon the leader took one by the ear and bawled at him and the others to 'Shut up'. After he had obtained some sort of order by shouts and threats the leader set up a few dilapidated games tables and did his best to get the youngsters occupied.

Don and the two young helpers (another had now arrived) all offered to help but were simply left standing around while

the leader continued his crude and not very successful efforts to maintain order.

When closing time arrived and the young people had gone, the two young helpers inquired, 'Didn't we agree to have a staff committee meeting to consider future plans for the club?' 'Oh, well, if we must,' was the response, 'though I don't see much point.' With no formal opening, minutes of a previous meeting or agenda he suddenly launched into an attack on 'them' – meaning mainly the minister and deacons. 'They never come and see what's happening, nor ask me,' he accused. 'Mark you, I wouldn't want them anyway. All I do this for is to get some experience so that the local authority will take me on as a youth leader.' After some aimless talk about the future they went home.

At the next deacons meeting someone, under 'Any Other Business', raised the question of the youth club. This led to heated discussion, with various complaints being levelled against the club and especially the leader, though no one knew enough about the situation at first hand to be sure which complaints were true and which untrue. The diaconate decided eventually that unless there was better order in the club within a month it would be closed down and that the church secretary should write and tell the Leader of this decision.

The letter was so ambiguous, however, that the leader thought that he was being dismissed but that the club was to continue. This produced a violent response, whereupon the church secretary wrote again more clearly.

The church secretary received a reply to say that when the leader was asked to take the job on, they had said he could do it indefinitely, and he was going to carry on as long as he wanted, whatever they said . . .

FAULTS AND DEFICIENCIES DETECTED:

1. The minister was not following any sensible procedure in making appointments.

Being a Christian Leader

GROUP TRAINING COURSE

CONTENTS

Introduction

1. This additional material, for use in a group training course on Christian leadership, is provided in the belief that many **benefits could come from working through this manual with others**; learning from, encouraging and challenging each other. It will not be possible for all who use this manual to share in such a group course. But if a course can be arranged in your church or Baptist Association, then we warmly commend its value, both for those on the course and the church or churches in which they serve.

2. There are **eight sessions** in the course, with ideally **a further introductory meeting** in which the group members get to know one another, covenant with one another to both see the course through and contribute to its success, and agree such practical matters as how often and where the group will meet.

You may agree to meet once a week for eight consecutive weeks. Fortnightly meetings may prove more convenient. In some cases there will be opportunity to spend a whole weekend together, working through the course in a more concentrated way. Group members must agree among themselves what is best for them and the course leader.

3. **A course leader needs to be appointed** by the church. The leader should have some understanding of leadership training, of management and of Baptist church life, and needs to possess sufficient teaching ability to lead the course satisfactorily and beneficially. The leader should be in a position to give time to study the subject and to be thoroughly prepared for each session.

If there is not a suitable person in your church, perhaps someone could be invited in from another church. Perhaps the Baptist Association to which your church belongs could be encouraged to train some people who would be available to the churches for this purpose.

The course leader, on request to the CTP office, Baptist House in Didcot, will be supplied with **an additional handbook containing guidelines and further material**.

4. What should be **the role of the minister** of the church in relation to this course? Both the church and the minister will profit from her/him being aware of what the course teaches (even, maybe, becoming a member of the course group!). However, this could inhibit the full participation of the course members who might tend to look too much to the minister for comment!

But a minister who is sufficiently well equipped could lead the course, and, in some circumstances, this may be necessary or desirable. The issue will have to be resolved as seems best in each church situation.

5. **The ideal size of the course group** is 12. If a church can muster only a few, the number might be made up by combining with another church, or the local Association might be approached to run the course for a number of churches together. The minimum number in the group should be 6 and the maximum number, 16. If too many apply, a further course could be arranged at a later date.

6. **To enable a church's leaders or potential leaders to share in this training course**, it may be necessary to reduce their duties for the eight weeks, or even to reduce the church activities themselves for that time. This may not be easy, but would be worth it in the long run. If some deacons can join the course, so much the better.

7. Before attending each session, course members should **study the material in the relevant unit** and the agenda for that session.

8. **The timing of the sessions** are guides and it may be that, in order to meet more effectively the needs of your group, you will agree with other members and the course leader to amend the suggested timings of the periods in each session. Flexibility in the timing and the agenda of each session must be a very clear option.

9. While the course is concerned with training individuals, the church should be the eventual recipient of its benefits and value. It will be important, therefore, that at the end of the eight sessions **the group compiles a report for the church's diaconate to consider**. The report could describe in sensitive, tactful and constructive tones the lessons learned from the course and ways in which the church's life and mission, through its organisation and committees, may be strengthened and improved.

If more than one church is involved, the course leader will need to arrange for one from each church to take back a report to his or her deacons.

GROUP TRAINING COURSE

Session 1

Setting the Scene

Period 1. (40 minutes)
Review of material in Unit 1 led by the course leader. Before coming to the session, read through Unit 1. What points were especially helpful and relevant for you? Use the TO THINK ABOUT sections to reflect on the issues raised in this unit.

Period 2. (35 minutes)

Lessons in Leadership

This is a role play exercise, exploring the need for leadership and how leadership emerges. If there are more than eight members, divide into two groups.

You are a group of individuals, unknown to each other until a few moments ago when you happened to meet on this remote and boggy part of Dartmoor after walking on a November afternoon. Fog has recently descended, leaving a visibility of no more than 50 metres. You all left any signs of roads and habitation over 20 minutes ago, and no one now knows exactly where you are – even though one of you has an OS map!

Among your possessions are the following: The OS map of Dartmoor, compass, six cheese sandwiches, two cans of Coke, three plastic raincoats, a back-pack with a small tent (big enough for two, three at a push), a bottle of TCP, a long bandage, two small plasters, three watches, three walking sticks.

One of your party (decide who before you begin the role play) has just stepped in a hole and sprained his/her ankle and cannot bear weight on it! One of you (again decide who) thinks you heard a church clock strike 3pm about 10 minutes ago.

You have to decide on:

a) What immediate action you should take to try to extricate yourselves from this predicament.
b) What contingency plans you should make for sheltering overnight.

Period 3. (40 minutes)
Come out of role and discuss together the questions asked by the leader.

Evaluation of this session
What did you learn from this session?

What did you find an obstacle to learning?

What particular aspect was helpful?

What action will you take as a result of the session?

GROUP TRAINING COURSE

Session 2

What the Bible says

Period 1. (40 minutes)
Review of material in Unit 2 led by course leader. Before coming to the session, read through Unit 2. What points were especially helpful and relevant for you? Use the TO THINK ABOUT sections to reflect on the issues raised in this unit.

Period 2. (20 minutes)
In a later session, attention is paid to various styles of leadership. But given what you know already, gather the names of about five Old Testament leaders. What word(s) would you use to describe the type of leadership you attribute to each? Using a flip chart, group members note what they think are the strengths and weaknesses of each type of Old Testament leader.

It may help the group if some members were prepared to sculpture with their bodies the different styles of leadership. What position would you place your body in, what gestures would you use, or how would you group yourself with others, to describe each style of leadership?

What are the similarities and differences in leadership styles between these Old Testament characters and Jesus?

Period 3. (20 minutes)

Lessons from the Jerusalem Conference

Read aloud Acts 15: 1–29. Members of the group could read particular parts of the passage; the narrative sections; the voices of Peter, James and the crowd; and the letter to the Gentile believers.

Now find answers to the following questions:

1. Is it obvious from this passage that leadership was necessary and given? If so, where?
2. Were the aims of this conference stated or implied? What were they?
3. Do you detect in this passage that flexibility and adaptation were present in the early church? If so, where?
4. Is there any evidence of a servant attitude among the leaders? If so, where?
5. Where, if at all, is the presence of team leadership evident?
6. There is no mention of James or the elders actually being appointed to their positions of leadership. Do you think that they would have come to their positions without careful and prayerful thought and acceptance on the part of others around them? Why do you answer as you do?

Period 4. (30 minutes)
Suggest some ways in which the six Biblical principles of Christian leadership (pages 14–20) could be applied more effectively in your church.

Begin by sharing in groups of two, then groups of four. Finally share your findings with the whole group, recording them on a flip chart.

> By the time you reach the next session, the course leader should have encouraged the group members to visit and observe a typical meeting of one or more of the church organisations or committees.
>
> An end result of the next session will be some recommendations (gentle and tactful!) to these organisations about possible improvements or changes to further their aims.

Evaluation of this session

What did you learn from this session?

What did you find an obstacle to learning?

What particular aspect was helpful?

What action will you take as a result of the session?

GROUP TRAINING COURSE

Session 3

Leaders' Responsibilities

In this session it is assumed you have had the opportunity to visit one or more organisations, groups or committees in your church. At the end of the session you will be able to suggest changes which may lead to the organisations' aims being better fulfilled.

Period 1. (40 minutes)
Review of material in Unit 3 led by the course leader. Before coming to the session, read through Unit 3. What points were especially helpful and relevant for you? Use the TO THINK ABOUT sections to reflect on the issues raised in this unit.

Period 2. (35 minutes)

Taking Stock

Divide into groups. Ensure that as far as possible various organisations, church groups and committees are represented in each group.

If there are members of more than one church on the course, it might be useful to divide into groups based on each church.

The aim of the exercise is to highlight the need for regular and thorough reviewing of the life, work and activities of a church.

Each group should consider the questions in one or more of the following sections. If a group covers more than one section, allocate a block of time to the first, then move on to the next. You may not deal with the questions thoroughly, but the exercise is not intended to result in final solutions to all your church's needs!

Section A. **Foster maximum unity in the church**

Q.1. Are there satisfactory arrangements in your church to ensure that the organisations and committees work co-operatively together? Yes/Partly/No.

Q.2. How well, *in practice*, do they pull together? Well/Fairly well/Poorly.

Q.3 Is there a means of bringing under one 'umbrella' those who work in similar fields. Yes/Partly/No.

Q.4. By what methods do the minister and deacons know what happens in each organisation, group and committee?

How well do they work? Well/Fairly well/Poorly.

Q.5. What else should you discuss on fostering unity in the church?

Section B. **Achieving aims and objectives**

Q.1. What are the aims and objectives of your church? Are they clearly defined and do they unite the church? If none have been formulated suggest some possibilities yourselves.

Q.2. What are the aims and objectives of the church organisations and committees whose affairs are known to you (list them)? If none have been formulated suggest some yourselves.

Section C. Work within structures and practices

Q.1. Has the church ever produced an Organisation Chart (see Unit 3, Section C.2)? Whether it has – or hasn't – produce a rough one yourselves, including in it all the organisations and committees.

Q.2. List arguments for and against the practice of congregational church government: its advantages and disadvantages.

Section D. Plan ahead.

Q.1. How regularly and constructively do you think your church plans ahead? Well/Fairly well/Poorly.

Q.2. What plans has the church in hand for six months ahead?

Q.3. What issues/plans should be priorities on the church's agenda over the next three years?

Q.4. Answer the same questions in relation to the organisations and committees whose affairs are known to you.

Section E. Efficient administration

Q.1. How efficient and effective is your church administration? Good/Fairly good/Poor.

Q.2. Ask the same question of the organisations and committees whose affairs are known to you.

Q.3. Where does the greatest administrative need lie in your church and its organisations?

Section F. Reviewing

Q.1. When last was the life and work of your church reviewed?

Q.2. Ask the same question of the organisations and committees whose affairs are known to you.

Q.3. How would you set about persuading an organisation that a Review would be useful?

Period 3. (30 minutes)
Come together for a brainstorming session, with members making *suggestions for improvement* in the functioning of their church, its organisations and committees.

In brainstorming, everyone is encouraged to call out suggestions as ideas occur to them. The leader records them immediately on a flip chart in order to categorise them later and include them in the suggested report to the deacons.

All course members should feel free to make any suggestion from the top of their heads, however crazy they may seem, and without any comment from others. Some of the best suggestions come from 'throw-away' thoughts, though there may well be some useless ones too!

Once again, you may not have time to do it thoroughly, but you will learn the method and value of brainstorming, which is one object of the exercise. At the same time the leader may collect some useful ideas to pass on to the deacons. If any group members feel that they have still more things to suggest, they can submit them to the leader in writing.

Evaluation of this session

What did you learn from this session?

What did you find an obstacle to learning?

What particular aspect was helpful?

What action will you take as a result of the session?

Session 4

Pulling Together

Period 1. (40 minutes)
Review of material in Unit 4 led by course leader. Before coming to the session, read through Unit 4. What points were especially helpful and relevant for you? Use the TO THINK ABOUT sections to reflect on the issues raised in this unit.

Period 2. (35 minutes)

All for One and One for All

This game involves members of the group inter-acting with each other to solve a problem. You will need eight participants; if there are other members of the group they may act as observers, together with the leader.

The leader will mark out a square with nine smaller squares inside it. The smaller squares will have a card placed in each, bearing a number from 1–8. The centre square will be clear. The eight appointed members will each be given a number 1–8 and will then stand in their appropriate square, holding their numbered card for all to see.

The exercise involves the eight players moving, one at a time, one space at a time, only moving backwards, forwards, or sideways (no diagonal movement) until the positions in the drawing on the left below become the positions in the right-hand drawing.

8	4	6
5		2
3	1	7

1	2	3
4	5	6
7	8	

No square may be occupied by more than one person. You must not swap cards! The leader will indicate whether verbal communication is allowed or whether only non-verbal communication is permitted.

At the end of the exercise group members discuss what they learned from the experience about different leadership styles and working as a team. The leader will put some questions to the group and any 'observers' may make comment.

Period 3. (45 minutes)

Get Your Act Together

a) **A role play** (5 minutes)
Two group members should act the characters in the role play below.

The minister has been deputed by the deacons to tell Mr A that he should relinquish his position as Sunday School Superintendent:

Min. Well Mr A it's very good of you to come on such a lovely evening as this. How is your garden looking?
Mr A Oh, not too bad; but you haven't got me here to talk about my garden have you?
Min. Well, not really. As a matter of fact the deacons asked me to have a chat with you about your position as Sunday School Superintendent.

Mr A Oh, so they've been talking about me behind my back. I'm surprised you and the deacons know what goes on in Sunday School. You've never been very interested before. What did they say?

Min. Well, they much appreciate so much of what you have done, but . . .

Mr A Oh yes, I expected there would be a 'but' somewhere. I can use 'buts' too. I may have my faults, but you must agree that the Sunday School was a shambles when I took it over. No one knew what they were supposed to do, nor where they should be located, nor how to teach, nor was there much modern equipment, and the discipline was terrible.

Min. Yes, Mr A, I must admit that, according to what they say – and perhaps we haven't kept in touch as we should – you have made great improvements with more boys and girls and greater efficiency since you took over, but you see . . .

Mr A Ah, another 'but'. What is it this time?

Min. Well, while you have made many changes for the better, the teachers are very unhappy about the way you treat them; they say you are rather high-handed, and now some of them are talking about resigning. It's that that the deacons are concerned about.

Mr A If people don't like being pushed to get to church in time to get the rooms ready, or to have preparation classes, or to commit themselves fully to the job, maybe they ought to resign. I've always believed that Christ deserves the best, and I've tried to give it.

Min. But what shall we do if they resign?

Mr A Recruit some more. There must be some other people about who would do it. I handle people very well at work. Why should they be so touchy in church?

Min. Well, I don't like to upset you, but I must say I was most disturbed when Mrs Brown came to me in tears over something you had said, and she, too, with all the trouble she has at home.

Mr A Perhaps I did go over the top a bit there, but I do these things with the best of intentions you know, and I have to think of the running of the Sunday School. And what would you do for another Sunday School Superintendent if you gave me the sack. Not many would take it on if you treated me like that. Not that it would worry me that much; as a matter of fact we've been thinking about changing churches.

Min. We wouldn't want that to happen, I'm sure. I wonder if we ought to think about this in the diaconate again . . .

b) **Discussion** (25 minutes)

Discuss the following questions, which relate to the Sections in Unit 4. Use a flip chart to record lessons learned.

1. What do you learn from this conversation about the deficiencies in the minister, deacons and Mr A in respect of their:
   a) Working in a team?
   b) Styles of leadership?
   c) Meeting the three areas of need?
   d) Motivating others?
2. What should have been done, or attempted, by minister and deacons before ever the situation reached this impasse?

c) **Take Two** (15 minutes)

Now role play the situation again, with two other course members taking the parts. This time, build into the conversation the lessons learned by the group in the discussion, showing how the conversation could have been handled more productively.

Afterwards, note and affirm the lessons which were incorporated into the re-run of the role play, and note any which were missing.

Evaluation of this session

What did you learn from this session?

What did you find an obstacle to learning?

What particular aspect was helpful?

What action will you take as a result of the session?

GROUP TRAINING COURSE

Session 5

Good Companions—Great Colleagues

Period 1. (40 minutes)
Review of material in Unit 5 led by course leader. Before coming to the session, read through Unit 5. What points were especially helpful and relevant for you? Use the TO THINK ABOUT sections to reflect on the issues raised in this unit.

Period 2. (40 minutes)

What Would *You* Do?

The following case studies, relating to the Sections in Unit 5, call for action.

Divide into groups of three or four people. Each group should answer the question, 'What would *you* do?' in respect of the case described. One case is allotted to each group. If there are fewer than four groups, choose which cases should be dealt with or agree that one or two groups look at more than one case.

Each group should have a sheet from a flip chart, or some other large sheet of paper. On this can be listed the group's responses to the questions.

Section 1. Beneficial relationships

A church Missions Committee is responsible for initiating action or recommending action to the church in support of both the Baptist Missionary Society and the Home Mission Fund.

On the committee is Miss B who is an enthusiastic supporter of the BMS and strongly believes that it should have its own separate supporting committee in the church. Mr C, also on the committee, is a keen promoter of HMF interests and equally strongly believes this should have its separate committee. Two other committee members are not particularly pro-Baptist and want to introduce support of inter-denominational missionary societies, whilst the remainder of the committee want to retain the status quo. Ill-will is being generated through this and progress in the committee is being hindered.

The Chairperson turns to you for advice on how to handle it. What actions would you recommend to him/her, and what dangers warn to avoid? Why would you propose these actions?

Section 2. Managing change

The minister wants to disband the traditional choir which has existed for many years. Most of its members are elderly and the maximum attending is ten. Its rendering of introits and anthems is becoming the cause of embarrassment or, especially among the young people, amusement. The attendance of young people at evening service is declining. The minister, who is musical, would like to form an orchestra of young people for use during the services, especially on Sunday evenings, believing this would improve the worship and help reverse the decline in church attendance. The choir, most of whom are loyal church members of long-standing, are positively hostile to the idea, even though the minister has discussed it sensitively with them.

You are the diaconate. Assuming that you are basically very much in favour of the change but prepared to modify it to reduce ill-will and perhaps worse, what would you recommend to the Church Meeting and why? What actions should be taken before the Church Meeting to help matters? How should the proposal to make the change be introduced to and handled in the Church Meeting? What actions should be taken after the Church Meeting?

Section 3. Education and training

There has never been any formal training of leaders or potential leaders in your church and, indeed, very little briefing before people have taken up jobs. There seems to be an indifference to it in the church generally. But you are a group of people who have awoken to the need for training.

What would you do to persuade the deacons and the church generally of the need for it. If they asked you to put it into effect what would you do? How, when and where would you do it?

Section 4. Delegate responsibilities

Yours is a growing church with a lay pastor and 100 members of a wide age-range and backgrounds. About 20 people are doing most of the work, i.e. administration, Sunday School teaching (30 children), stewarding, cleaning and caretaking; 5 of these are also deacons – who include the church secretary and treasurer. Most of them have secular jobs as well.

There is an obvious need for such as a mothers and toddlers group, a luncheon club, youth activities, pastoral care groups, evangelistic and social outreach and house groups.

You are the diaconate. What practical actions would you propose so as to share out the present work and increasingly meet the needs of the people in and outside the church? How would you go about implementing that action?

Period 3. (40 minutes)
Each group should share its findings. Discussion and further comment will follow. The sheets of paper, with the groups' conclusions, can be pinned to a wall for all to see.

Evaluation of the session

What did you learn from this session?

What did you find an obstacle to learning?

What particular aspect was helpful?

What action will you take as a result of the session?

GROUP TRAINING COURSE

Session 6

Close Encounters

Period 1. (40 minutes)
Review of material in Unit 6 led by course leader. Before coming to the session, read through Unit 6. What points were especially helpful and relevant for you? Use the TO THINK ABOUT sections to reflect on the issues raised in this unit.

Period 2. (20 minutes)

Getting the Message.

Do the exercise on page 54 on the transmission and reception of information.

Period 3. (30 minutes)

A Decision-making Simulation.

Imagine yourselves as your church's diaconate. You are having to decide on the following matter and take a recommendation to the Church Meeting. Someone from the group should act as chairperson.

The young people's organisations are: Two Sunday morning groups, one of 12–14 year-olds and another of 15–18s, 'After-Eight Fellowship' on Sunday evenings for 13–20s, weeknight Youth Fellowship, Scout Group, and Girls' Brigade Company.

Unfortunately these have little or no contact with each other, except when they find that they want to meet at the same time and in the same location, or they use each other's equipment without permission. All this creates persistent resentment and ill-will.

The minister and church secretary bring the following proposition to the diaconate:

> We recommend to the Church Meeting that John Smith be appointed as Youth Director in order to unite the youth work and harmonise relationships.'

When you get the agenda you quickly see that the proposition is too brief and ill-defined as it stands. Also they have forgotten that one of the difficulties, among others, is that Scout groups are to some extent under the authority of the local Scout District. This proposal will obviously cause much questioning, discussion and, no doubt, argument in the Deacons' and Church Meetings and make the situation worse than it is. Yet you know that something should be done.

On the diaconate are 'interested parties' in the persons of the Scout Leader (Billy Bruiser), the Sunday School Superintendent (Simon Stodge) and a married couple (Peter Pious and Penelope Prim) who run the Youth Fellowship. (The leader will appoint beforehand group members to take on these roles during the discussion.)

The diaconate has to frame a resolution which it can recommend to the Church Meeting to remedy the present problems and advance the youth work generally.

Period 4. (30 minutes)
Still within the roles, discuss how well the meeting went and, from the perspective of your character in the role play, what you think was achieved.

Then step out of role.

The course leader will have acted as observer of this decision-making exercise. He or she will now make an assessment and evaluation of how it was conducted based on questions in the Handbook for Leaders. *You must be able to tolerate and profit from this appraisal and any implied criticism that may result.*

Members of the group should also share their observations and assessments.

List on a flip chart the learning from the exercise which is relevant for your church's situation.

Evaluation of this session

What did you learn from this session?

What did you find an obstacle to learning?

What particular aspect was helpful?

What action will you take as a result of the session?

GROUP TRAINING COURSE

Session 7

What Good Leaders Are Made Of

Period 1. (40 minutes)
Review of material in Unit 7 led by the course leader. Before coming to the session, read through Unit 7. What points were especially helpful and relevant for you? Use the TO THINK ABOUT sections to reflect on the issues raised in this unit.

Period 2. (35 minutes)

Personal Appraisal Exercise.

Members of the group complete the following questionnaire, designed to identify abilities and gifts which may at present be hidden or unrecognised, either by themselves or others.

It is important to fill in the columns on pages 90–93 before looking at page 94!

In column a give yourself marks from 1 to 5, according to how true you think the statements are of you.

If very slightly true give yourself 1
If slightly true give yourself 2
If moderately true give yourself 3
If largely true give yourself 4
If very largely true give yourself 5

Do not think over-long about any question.

It can be useful to find out the opinions of your friends about the abilities and gifts which God has given you! *But, do NOT do so unless your friendship with them is strong enough to withstand implied criticism!!* If it is, invite up to three of them to complete columns b, c, and d. If they do it on a separate form to your own so much the better, as they will not be influenced by your answers.

If the course members have developed sufficient trust and confidence in each other, and providing they know one another fairly well, then each member could submit to the honest assessment of other members of the group.

Generally speaking, how true is it that:

		a	b	c	d
1.	I am good at listening.				
2.	I can easily get people to understand what I am saying.				
3.	People in a group usually listen carefully to what I say.				
4.	I readily listen to those whose opinions differ from mine.				
5.	I like planning ahead.				
6.	I wish I could do more to relieve the needs of people in my neighbourhood.				
7.	I often visualise myself leading Sunday worship.				
8.	I can easily hold conversations with young people.				
9.	I find it easy to get co-operation from children.				
10.	I tend to take the lead in most groups I am in.				

		a	b	c	d
11.	I long to help and heal people as Jesus did.				
12.	I am ready of speech.				
13.	People easily grasp the meaning of what I say.				
14.	I want to be involved in bringing individuals to faith in Christ.				
15.	I am good at organising events.				
16.	I take a close interest in politics and social affairs.				
17.	I am good at reading in public.				
18.	Young people talk to me readily.				
19.	Children take to me easily.				
20.	I am an adventurous type.				
21.	I can sense when people are in need of help.				
22.	I enjoy study.				
23.	I like explaining difficult things to people.				
24.	I am patient with those who are antagonistic to the Christian faith.				
25.	I find it easy to attend to detail.				
26.	When I see a down-and-out I wish I could help.				
27.	Other people often find my spoken prayers helpful.				
28.	I feel at ease with most young people.				
29.	I am fond of children – even the naughty ones.				
30.	People tend to follow my suggestions.				
31.	I find it easy to be tactful.				
32.	I find the Bible a rewarding book to study.				
33.	I have plenty of self-confidence.				
34.	I am patient but persistent with those unresponsive to the Gospel.				
35.	I keep my possessions and papers tidy, and in order.				
36.	I find myself doing lots of practical things for others.				
37.	I enjoy participating in worship as a member of the congregation.				
38.	I am fond of young people, even when they misbehave.				
39.	Children easily understand what I am telling them.				
40.	I enjoy organising people and events.				
41.	I have lots of patience.				
42.	I have an urge to speak about Christ and the Gospel to as many as possible.				
43.	I find it easy to stand up before an audience.				
44.	I have a genial nature.				
45.	I don't usually lose or mislay things.				

		a	b	c	d
46.	I want to work to bring justice and peace to society.				
47.	I would love to help lead people to a deep sense of worship at the Sunday services.				
48.	Even rebellious young people usually do what I ask.				
49.	I would like to give more help in children's activities.				
50.	I find it easy to delegate work to others.				
51.	The advice I give to those in trouble is usually reliable.				
52.	I enjoy thinking out what I would like to tell a congregation.				
53.	I want to know the Bible well enough to explain it to others.				
54.	I relate easily to people.				
55.	I can accurately assess other people's abilities.				
56.	People often come to me for help.				
57.	I can readily convey my sense of worship to others.				
58.	I wish the churches did much more for the more difficult young people.				
59.	I want to introduce lots of children to Jesus.				
60.	People often ask for my opinion on difficult questions.				
61.	I have a good understanding of most human problems.				
62.	I can easily hold the attention of even a large group of people.				
63.	I like unravelling the meaning of the more difficult parts of the Bible.				
64.	I soon get into conversation with strangers.				
65.	I can maintain friendly relations even when I am under stress.				
66.	I like to help with such as flag-days and house-to-house collections.				
67.	I am soon in a spirit of worship on Sundays.				
68.	I would love to help more young people develop into fine Christians.				
69.	I am able to get down to children's level when talking to them.				
70.	I like a challenge.				
71.	I can cover up shock when people confess their misbehaviour to me.				
72.	I have clear diction.				
73.	I have lots of patience when explaining things to people.				
74.	I find it easy to speak personally to others of Christ.				
75.	I can tell when an event or organisation is going well.				
76.	I contribute generously to good causes.				
77.	I am able to convey an attitude of self-confidence, even when a lot of people are looking at me.				
78.	I find it easy to understand young people.				
79.	I wish I could be more involved in helping families with problems.				

		a	b	c	d
80.	I don't easily give up in face of difficulties.				
81.	I seem to be able to lift people up whose faith is low.				
82.	I have a strong voice.				
83.	I can present my thoughts in orderly fashion.				
84.	Non-Christians seem to find it easy to get into discussion with me about religion.				
85.	I am good at keeping a forward diary and keeping engagements on time.				
86.	I wish the churches were giving more practical care to the needy.				
87.	People easily hear what I say when I speak publicly.				
88.	I find it satisfying to be with young people.				
89.	I find it easy to hold children's attention.				
90.	I take good note of other people's suggestions.				
91.	People seem to want to tell me their troubles.				
92.	I can present my ideas in a methodical and comprehensible fashion.				
93.	I try to persuade Christians of the importance of Christian education.				
94.	I am able to sense how people are feeling.				
95.	I answer business letters promptly.				
96.	I am a great admirer of such as Martin Luther King, Mother Theresa, Dr Barnardo and Lord Shaftesbury.				
97.	I have an agreeable way of expressing myself.				
98.	I feel sorry for the young people aimlessly roaming our streets.				
99.	I can readily express myself in simple language.				
100.	My decision-making is quick and good.				

Now turn to the analysis chart on the next page. Insert the figures from column a of the questions sheet into the corresponding boxes and columns of the chart. For example, insert the figure given for question 1 into the box numbered 1 and under column a, and so on. If any questions are unanswered insert the figure 3 for calculation purposes. Add up each column a.

If you asked friends or other members of the course group to complete the questionnaire, then repeat the process for columns b, c, d from the valuations given by them.

The totals of column a, under each of sections A to J in the chart, indicate how strong you think yourself to be in the ability areas listed below. (Any total above 30 marks gives an above-average assessment.)

A.	PASTORAL CARING	F.	SERVING THE COMMUNITY
B.	PREACHING	G.	HELPING TO LEAD IN WORSHIP
C.	TEACHING	H.	WORKING WITH YOUNG PEOPLE
D.	PERSONAL WITNESSING	I.	WORKING WITH CHILDREN
E.	ORGANISING AND ADMINISTRATING	J.	NATURAL LEADERSHIP

If others gave their assessment, take the average of the totals of columns b, c, and d for each section and compare it with the mark given by yourself; this may throw further light on what abilities you truly have.

The result of this exercise will only be a rough guide, but may well give some indication where and how God can use you.

ANALYSIS CHART

Pastoral caring	Preach-ing	Teach-ing	Personal Witnessing	Organising and Admin.	Serving Com-munity	Help Lead Worship	Young People	Children	Leader-ship
A	B	C	D	E	F	G	H	I	J
a b c d	a b c d	a b c d	a b c d	a b c d	a b c d	a b c d	a b c d	a b c d	a b c d
1	2	3	4	5	6	7	8	9	10
11	12	13	14	15	16	17	18	19	20
21	22	23	24	25	26	27	28	29	30
31	32	33	34	35	36	37	38	39	40
41	42	43	44	45	46	47	48	49	50
51	52	53	54	55	56	57	58	59	60
61	62	63	64	65	66	67	68	69	70
71	72	73	74	75	76	77	78	79	80
81	82	83	84	85	86	87	88	89	90
91	92	93	94	95	96	97	98	99	00
T									
Av.____	Av.____	Av.____	Av.____	Av.____	Av.____	Av.____	Av.____	Av.____	Av.____

Period 3. (35 minutes)

Appointment Procedure Exercise

In groups of two or three, draw up the job specification for a mutually agreed leadership task in your church. The small groups may choose different tasks.

After 15 minutes, come together as a group and share the job specifications and why you have included the various points.

Record your findings on a flip chart.

Evaluation of the session

What did you learn from this session?

What did you find an obstacle to learning?

What particular aspect was helpful?

What action will you take as a result of the session?

GROUP TRAINING COURSE

Session 8

Preparing and Supporting Leaders

Period 1. (40 minutes)
Review of material in Unit 8 led by course leader. Before coming to the session, read through Unit 8. What points were especially helpful and relevant for you? Use the TO THINK ABOUT sections to reflect on the issues raised in this unit.

Period 2. (30 minutes)

Spotting the Deficiencies

Course members *individually* do the exercise on page 11. If this exercise was attempted near the beginning of the course, then it will be worthwhile noting any changes of perception, due to things learned during the course.

Period 3. (30 minutes)
The leader takes the members through the exercise text a paragraph at a time, seeking agreement on the faults and deficiencies. (15 minutes)

In groups of two or three discuss what one or more of these interested parties should do to remedy the defects and avoid them in the future: the minister, deacons, Church Meeting, Youth Club leader and assistant leaders. (15 minutes)

Period 4. (15 minutes)
A short brainstorming session in which the members suggest some of the points which the course leader should make in his report to the deacons and/or elders of the church or churches to which the course members belong.

Evaluation of this session

What did you learn from this session?

What did you find an obstacle to learning?

What particular aspect was helpful?

What action will you take as a result of the session?

COURSE EVALUATION

1. In what ways has this course helped you in your development as a person and as a Christian?

2. In what ways has the course helped to develop any skills needed for specific leadership tasks?

3. What three things in the course have you found particularly useful?

4. What have you found unhelpful or disappointing in either the content of the course or the process (the way it was structured)?

5. What three major pieces of action will you take as a result of the course?

6. Would the leader allow the group to evaluate his or her contribution to the course? If so, what was the group's assessment of that contribution – its strengths and weaknesses?

In the interests of improving this material, it would be helpful if you would share your evaluation of this course with the CTP Office at the Baptist Union, PO Box 44, 129 Broadway, Didcot, Oxon. OX11 8RT.

APPENDIX A

(see Unit 6 Section C.)

ARRANGING AND CONDUCTING A WOMEN'S DEVOTIONAL MEETING

Though these guidelines are designed mainly with women's meetings in mind, it can be adapted for use by any church group.

1. THE PROGRAMME IS PLANNED

The committee of the organisation (e.g. the officers, leaders, plus one or two others from the meeting) will in good time plan the programme for the next session.

2. THE SECRETARY

a. Immediate Action

- Following the programme planning meeting make all necessary arrangements in respect of the venue, speakers, and any other participants, working closely with the leader in this.
- Ensure (in writing ideally) that they – especially the speaker – are fully aware of what is expected of them, and know the date, time and type of meeting place – and how to get there.
- Remind the speaker (and any other participant, if applicable) approximately a week before the engagement.

b. Before the meeting

- Prepare Notices.
- Arrive in good time. See that the room is arranged and as comfortable as possible and everything else in proper order.
- Check that the chairperson is fully conversant with the details of the programme.
- Ensure that the speaker (if any) is welcomed and looked after.
- Help everyone to feel at home.

c. During the Meeting

- Keep alert to any developments that need your attention so as to ensure its smooth running.
- Give out notices clearly, concisely and loudly!

d. After the Meeting

- Give courteous attention to the speaker (she/he needs a cup of tea too!)
- Make friendly contact with members.
- See that the room and premises are left in proper order.

3. THE LEADER/CHAIRPERSON

We are assuming that the overall leader of the organisation also chairs the meetings, though this is not necessarily so.

a. Before the Day of the Meeting

- Prepare for the meeting; e.g. arrange programme, hymns (if any), etc.
- See that any you have asked to take part are fully informed of what is expected of them.
- Always be prepared to take appropriate action if the speaker does not arrive.

b. Before the Meeting

- Arrive in good time. Check that all arrangements are well in hand and everyone who has responsibilities is taking them satisfactorily.
- Make everyone, including the speaker, feel welcome and at home on arrival.
- See that the speaker is fully aware of what is expected of her/him, and when.
- If hymns are to be sung see that the accompanist knows the numbers and tunes. Check that others taking part are aware of what is expected of them.
- Call the meeting to order *on time*.

c. During the Meeting

- Keep control kindly but firmly.
- Make sure you can be heard by all.
- Help create friendly atmosphere.
- Lead worship and prayer helpfully.
- See that the programme goes through smoothly.
- Introduce the speaker with proper courtesies, giving some background information about her/him (obtained beforehand).
- Close *on time*.

d. After the Meeting

- Give proper attention to the speaker (or get someone else to).
- Make friendly contact with the members.

4. THE TREASURER

The Treasurer should see that speakers' expenses are fully met. She will know how far a speaker has travelled and can calculate well enough the cost of public transport, or car expenses. The cost of petrol should at least be covered, but it shows appreciation to err on the side of generosity. The speaker should not be placed in the position of being asked her expenses (nor paid directly out of the collection!). The sum should be placed in an envelope and handed privately to the speaker at a convenient time during the gathering.

APPENDIX B
USEFUL RESOURCES

LITERATURE

1. FURTHER MATERIAL BY THE AUTHOR

Bacon, Fred, Workbooks: I *Planning Your Church's Programme,* II *Making the Most of People's Resources,* III *Getting Well Organised* (Bristol Baptist Association, 1987). Available from 8 Heath Road, Downend, Bristol BS16 6HA.

Church Administration (Baptist Union, 1990).

2. THEORY AND PRACTICE OF LEADERSHIP

Adair, John, *Effective Leadership* (Pan Books, 1983).

Baumohl, Anton, *Grow Your Own Leaders* (Scripture Union, 1987).

Clark, Stephen, *Know How to Use an Overhead Projector* (Scripture Union, 1985).

Copley, Derek, *Taking a Lead* (Kingsway, 1985).

Cormack, David, *Team Spirit* (Marc Europe, 1987).

King, Philip, *Leadership Explosion* (Hodder and Stoughton, 1987).

Lazell, David, *Know How – Video* (Scripture Union, 1984).

Pearson, Brian, *Yes Manager – management in the local church* (Grove Books, 1986).

Pierson, Lance, *Know How to Give a Five-Minute Talk* (Scripture Union, 1984).

3. WORKING WITH GROUPS

Baumohl, Anton, *Making Adult Disciples* (Scripture Union, 1984).

Cotterell, Peter, *All About House Groups* (Kingsway, 1985).

Evans, P., *What? Me a Housegroup Leader?* (Grove Books, 1984).

Kindred, Michael, *Once upon a group* (Michael Kindred, 1984, obtainable from: 20 Dover St., Southwell, Notts, NG25 0EZ).

Mallison, John, *Building Small Groups* (Scripture Union, 1978).

Mallison, John, *Growing Christians in Small Groups* (Scripture Union, 1989).

Parker, Margaret, *Leading Groups* (Epworth Press, 1987).

Roberts, Keith, *Small Groups in the Church* (Kingsway, 1990).

4. PASTORAL CARE

Fowke, Ruth, *Beginning Pastoral Counselling* (Grove Books, 1985).

Jacobs, Michael, *Swift to Hear* (SPCK, 1985).

Rackley, John, *Pastoral Care in the Local Church* (The Baptist Union).

Messenger, Ron, *Pastoral Counselling* (Baptist Union Christian Training Programme).

5. COMMUNICATION

Eyre, E.C., *Business Communication Made Simple* (Heinemann, 1987).

AGENCIES OFFERING RESOURCES AND TRAINING

Administry, 69 Sandridge Rd, St Albans, Herts, AL1 4AG – publish material, run courses, provide resources.

Bible Society, Stonehill Green, Westlea, Swindon, Wilts, SN5 7DG – produce a wide range of written, audio and visual resources, run courses.

Church Pastoral Aid Society, Falcon Court, 32 Fleet St, London, EC47 1DB. Audio–visual resources for training in leadership. Publish a magazine three times a year for home group leaders.

Marc Europe, Cosmos House, 6 Homesdale Rd, Bromley, Kent, BR2 9EX – publish material, run courses, provide resources.

Scripture Union Training Unit, 26–30 Heathcoat St, Nottingham, NG1 3AA – provide a wide range of courses, offer a consultancy service to churches, publish training material.

Star Training Resources Limited, Kelston Park Training Centre, Bath, Avon, BA1 9AE – offer residential, non-residential or on-the-spot training for churches in leadership, management and Christian education.

Trinity Training (Shân Dobinson), 3 Brook St, Wolston, Warwickshire, CV8 3HD – a management training consultancy, but also offers courses for Christians in, for example, management, leadership and time management.

Westhill College, Church Management Department, Weoley Park Road, Selly Oak, Birmingham, B29 6LL – offers courses in management and leadership.

APPENDIX C
SAMPLE DOCUMENTS

JOB DESCRIPTION

Organisation:	Mixed Youth Club (ages 15–21).
Key Objectives:	To provide social and recreational facilities in a Christian atmosphere, maintaining good though relaxed order, and seeking to influence the young people to become Christians and church members.
Position:	Assistant Leader
Duties:	*General* To foster the young people's enjoyment and to strengthen the Christian influence in the club. *Particular* To participate with the other leaders in arranging and organising club activities. To help other leaders and workers with the oversight of indoor games and outdoor pursuits. To take charge of ordering and retailing refreshments, keeping an account of the money. Stand in for the overall leader when required. Conduct occasional epilogues.
To whom responsible:	Club overall leader.
By whom appointed:	Club leaders in consultation with church leaders.
Term of appointment:	Appointment to be reviewed after one year. Thereafter it shall be for four years only, unless exceptional circumstances make an extension essential.

JOB-HOLDER'S SPECIFICATIONS

Taking the above assistant youth club leader's description as an example we can see what the job-holder's specification would be like. It could read as follows:

- A Christian of either sex.
- Preferably a member of the church or regular member of the congregation.
- Accepts the key objectives of the club.
- Preferably experienced in and trained for youth work but, in any case, with evident abilities for it.
- Responsible and reliable.
- Sensitive to the problems of young people today and how to relate to them helpfully.
- Fit enough physically to join in recreational activities.
- Able to take the lead and maintain discipline.
- Has some organisational competence.

CHURCH REVIEW

The following provide examples of documents which can be used to conduct the review of a church's activities. The questionnaire could be adapted for application to church committees or other groups.

FACTS SHEET FOR ORGANISATIONS

To be completed by leader(s) of

_____________________________ Organisation

Dear Leaders,

As no doubt you know, our church has agreed to engage in what we are calling a 'People's Resources Project'. This is to discover and use the abilities and other possessions of all our people in the way in which God wants, in order that the work and witness of our church prospers. It also should help to share the work more equitably among the membership.

In order to know how best to use any offers we receive, it is essential that we know what our organisations, committees and other activities need. We have arranged, therefore, for a Review to be made of the different sections of church life.

It would greatly help us if you, in company with your fellow workers, would complete this Facts Sheet. It should not take too long.

Later, one or two from the Project Committee will meet with you so that you may discuss with them the successes, difficulties, failures, prospects for the future, and consequent needs of your organisation.

We shall be most grateful for your kind co-operation.

With all good wishes.

_______________ _______________

Minister Project Organiser

Organisation leaders please complete in duplicate and return one copy to the Project Committee by:

If not clear on any point please consult a member of the Project Committee.

Use additional paper where necessary.

---

1. Which particular group of people do you mainly serve? (Please underline): a) Children (male, female), b) Young people (male, female), c) Adults (male, female).
2. Which age group do they chiefly fall into?
3. When and where do you meet?
4. Average attendance: *Male* *Female*
   This year:
   Last year:
   Year before:
5. What *specific objectives* do you have? Please give marks from 0 (low) to 5 (high) to those objectives listed below according to the prominence they receive in your organisation.

   We seek to:

   a. Provide recreation and fun ____
   b. Provide friendly contact with others ____
   c. Help members to understand and value the Christian faith ____
   d. Lead members to a personal commitment to Christ ____
   e. Encourage worship and prayer ____
   f. Foster Christian growth and behaviour ____
   g. Incorporate members into church life ____
   h. Equip members for service ____
   i. Give pastoral care to members ____
   j. Others . . . ____
6. What is *being done* in your programme, and by what methods and activities, to stimulate, encourage and help those who attend to:

   a. Have recreation and fun?
   b. Establish helpful friendships?
   c. Learn about the Christian faith?
   d. Attend Sunday worship?
   e. Commit themselves to Christ?
   f. Join in worship and prayer?
   g. Ask for baptism and church membership?

h. Grow as Christians?
i. Engage in Christian witnessing?
j. Support the denomination and wider church?
k. Increase their missionary interest and support?
l. Share their problems?

7. Number who are church members:
8. Number attending Sunday services.
   Never: Occasionally: Frequently:
9. Number becoming Christians.
   This year: Last year: Year before:
10. Number becoming church members.
    This year: Last year: Year before:
11. (For children's and youth work). What efforts are made to contact the parents who do not attend church?
12. Are there written Rules or Guidelines for your organisation?
13. Leaders and other staff:
    Names Position or Role
    a. How and by whom are the leaders and other staff appointed and for what term?
    b. What briefing or training do they receive for their job?
       i) Before appointment?
       ii) During service?
    c. Who are involved in making decisions on running the organisation?
    d. Do the leaders and staff meet regularly in committee?
14. During the past year what happenings have given you
    a. The most satisfaction?
    b. The most disappointments and problems?
15. What changes, if any, would you recommend, particularly in relation to Questions 1, 2, 3, 5, 6, 11, 12, 13?
16. What extra resources are needed in respect of:
    a. Personnel?
    b. Equipment, materials, accommodation?
    c. Finance?
    (Please remember that no promises can be made to you until we know what offers of extra help have been received.)
17. Any other comments?

TARGETS PLAN FOR YOUTH CLUB LEADERS

To be completed during the next twelve months.

1. *Attendance of members:* Increase numbers by 10%. Keep an attendance register. Contact any who have not attended for the past three meetings.
2. *Relationships among members:* Stamp out bullying and the formation of mini-gangs.
3. *Games and recreational facilities:* Increase these so that all who want to use them can be kept occupied.
4. *Attendance at church:* Increase by 10%.
5. *Commitment to Christ:* Encourage Christian club members to influence other members towards this. Leaders watch out for suitable opportunities for personal talks. Introduce features into the Epilogue which present the Gospel attractively and arrestingly so as to increase attention and attendance. Aim at seeing at least five young people won to Christ.
6. *Homes and families of members:* Try to make contact with those not attending church either by church literature, or personally, or both.
7. *Leaders and helpers:*
   a. Ensure proper time-keeping so that club is opened and closed on time.
   b. Keep to rota of duties in future, except

when impossible. Notify leader as soon as possible when unable to attend.

c. Those who have not yet taken Youth Leaders' Training Course do so. Encourage promising members of club to do the same.

d. Hold without fail monthly committee meetings when policy decisions will be taken jointly.

CHURCH HANDBOOK

Of value to all members of a church and congregation, especially when they first join the church is a Church Handbook giving a broad description of the church and its life. If for Baptists, it could cover such areas as:

1. The Baptists
2. How our church came into being
3. How our church is governed
4. Becoming a church member
5. Responsibilities of church membership
6. The place of baptism, the Lord's Supper, and special services
7. Relationships with other Baptists and other Christians
8. Our church today:
   - Sunday worship
   - Christian nurturing
   - Organisations, committees and other activities
   - Finances:
     - church expenses
     - church income
     - support of other causes
9. Our aims and hopes
10. List of all church activities
11. List of church members and associates

OFFERS AND REQUESTS CANVASS

The questionnaire gives an example of what could be included in a Canvass. There is probably little limit to the number of useful questions you might ask. But these should be restricted because a lengthy questionnaire might frighten people off from answering it! The following example should be adopted or adapted as is deemed best.

LETTER FROM MINISTER

Dear Friend,

You are invited to respond to the questions on the following pages so that our church can discover what personal abilities and other resources for Christian service might be available from our congregation. It may well be that this questionnaire will help you realise that you have resources to offer of which you were unaware.

No unfair pressure will be brought to bear as a result of your replies; indeed we are asking you at present to say only if you are prepared to *discuss* your offers with us, not make firm ones. Also, and we must stress this, we cannot promise to take up every offer of help; we may, for instance, have more offers in certain areas than we can actually use. But we shall acknowledge or follow up all of them, in due course.

We also give opportunity in the different sections below for you to make any particular *requests* for advice or help. We shall do what we can to meet them but we have to say that we cannot promise to be able to meet all the needs expressed, certainly not immediately, but we shall contact you about them in due course.

We shall greatly appreciate your help, and being able to help you.

Yours sincerely,

Minister *Project Organiser*

QUESTIONNAIRE

Name ____________

Address ____________

____________ Tel. ____________

Age (please underline the appropriate group):
Under 16, 16–19, 20–35, 36–50, 51–65, Over 65

Please indicate against the following items which offers you would like to discuss with a member of the Project Committee, and the requests you make. Please underline your responses.

You will not, thereby, be committing yourself to fulfil, if asked, the offers you indicate, but simply to discuss them. Therefore, please, underline all the offers that you are *interested* in.
Which, if any, will be taken up by the church will depend upon how many offers we get from other people and what seems best from discussion with you.

No one is expected to make offers under every section. Please remember, too, that even if you are able to make only *one* offer we would like to know about it.

(It will help if, under 'Offers' you underline also those items in which you are already engaged.)

If you want more information, please contact ____________

Please return this to ____________

as soon as convenient, but not later than ____________

1. **Sunday Services**

Offers: I would like to discuss:

1.1 Helping at Sunday worship by occasionally:

1.1.1 *a.* Reading the Scriptures *b.* Leading in prayer
1.1.2 Singing *a.* Individually *b.* In a choir
1.1.3 Playing a musical instrument (please state which)
1.1.4 Giving an address *a.* To children *b.* To adults
1.1.5 Writing *a.* Prose *b.* Poetry *c.* Music *d.* Drama
1.1.6 Participating in *a.* Drama productions *b.* Dance
1.1.7 Producing visual aids
1.1.8 Sharing in group preparation of worship
1.1.9 And . . .

1.2 Having my name on the rota for:

1.2.1 Opening and closing the church on Sunday *a.* Mornings *b.* Evenings
1.2.2 Welcoming people into church *a.* Mornings *b.* Evenings
1.2.3 Stewarding during the services *a.* Mornings *b.* Evenings
1.2.4 Preparing for and clearing away after Communion Services *a.* Mornings *b.* Evenings
1.2.5 *a.* Providing flowers for the church *b.* Arranging them

Requests:

1.1 I need transport in order to be able to get to church on Sunday *a.* Mornings *b.* Evenings

1.2 I am unable to attend church and would like to receive Communion at home

1.3 I would like to receive tapes of the services to play at home
1.4 I would like also . . .

2. Christian Nurture

Offers: I would like to discuss:

2.1 Joining a group for regular study, discussion and fellowship.
Suitable times would be:
a. Weekday mornings/afternoons/evenings
b. Sunday mornings/afternoons/evenings
I could meet *a.* on church premises *b.* in a home
2.2 Offering the use of my home for house groups
2.3 Organising a nurture group (state skills offered)
2.4 Offering also . . .

Requests:

2.1 I would like to receive Bible study notes and other helps for daily reading
2.2 I would like to know what is required if one is to become a member of this church
2.3 I would like also . . .

3. Prayer

Offers: I would like to discuss:

3.1 Joining a group for regular prayer.
Suitable times would be:
a. Weekday mornings/afternoons/evenings
b. Sunday mornings/afternoons/evenings
I could meet *i.* on church premises *ii.* in a home
3.2 Praying privately for those people and matters which are on the church prayer list (supplied on request)
3.3 Offering my home for prayer groups
3.4 Offering also . . .

Requests:

3.1 I would like the following to be included on the church prayer list:
3.2 I would like also . . .

4. Church Premises and Church Grounds

Offers: I would like to discuss:

4.1 Offering the following expertise/skills in maintenance of the premises and care of the grounds:

Requests:

4.1 The following improvements to the premises and facilities would help me benefit more from church worship and other activities.

5. Finance:

Offers: I would like to discuss:

5.1 Offering the following expertise/skills in relation to church finances:
5.2 Counting the Sunday offerings and taking them to the Bank

Requests:

5.1 I would like more details about the financial needs of the church and the causes it supports
5.2 I would like to talk over with someone how I can give most beneficial support to the church and other causes
5.3 I would like to receive a set of offering envelopes to help me give regularly to the church
5.4 I would like details about how to covenant my giving so that the church can recover income tax on my gift
5.5 I would like also . . .

6. Evangelistic Outreach

Offers: I would like to discuss:

6.1 Helping to *a.* Distribute leaflets *b.* Visit homes *c.* Organise evangelistic activities *d.* Join special prayer groups *e.* And . . .

Requests:

6.1 I would like someone to discuss with me the Christian faith and Christian growth.

7. Serving the Community

Offers: I would like to discuss:

7.1 Helping others by *a*. Child-minding *b*. Baby-sitting *c*. Providing occasional nursing help *d*. House maintenance *e*. Gardening *f*. Visiting homes for the elderly etc. *g*. Shopping for the house-bound *h*. Giving transport *i*. And . . .
7.2 Representing the church on local welfare committees

Requests:

7.1 I would like advice and, possibly, help on the following:

8. Equipment

Offers: I would like to discuss:

8.1 Lending occasionally the following equipment to the church (e.g. amplifying equipment, projector, video recorder, power tools, lawnmower, computer):
8.2 Operating equipment such as:

Requests:

8.1 It would be helpful if the church had the following equipment available for me and others when attending church (e.g. entrance ramp, wheel chair, walking frame):

9. Transport

Offers: I would like to discuss:

9.1 Transporting people to church regularly/occasionally. Possible times would be: *a*. Sunday mornings/evenings *b*. Week-day mornings/afternoons/evenings
9.2 Organising a transport rota
9.3 Driving the church minibus

Requests:

9.1 I would like transport to church regularly/occasionally on Sunday *a*. Mornings *b*. Evenings *c*. And/Or . . .

10. Pastoral Care

Offers: I would like to discuss:

10.1 Helping with *a*. Visiting people *b*. Counselling *c*. Caring for the sick *d*. The day centre *e*. Senior Citizens Club
10.2 Advising or helping people in practical matters
10.3 Serving on the Pastoral Committee
10.4 *a*. Occasionally providing meals *b*. Giving hospitality to people in need
10.5 And . . .

Requests:

10.1 Because I am a student/live alone/come from a distance/or . . . I would appreciate having *a*. Lunch *b*. Tea provided on Sundays regularly/occasionally
10.2 I would like a personal talk with the minister/or . . .
10.3 I would also like . . .

11. Church Activities

Offers: I would like to discuss:

11.1 Helping with the following church activities:
(Please underline in the following lists of organisations, committees, and other activities, those that you are already helping in or would consider doing so if needed.)
Organisations Committees Other Activities
11.2 My children attending the following church activities:
11.3 My attending the following church activities:

Requests:

11.1 Please send me further details of church activities which might suit *a*. My needs *b*. The needs of my children, aged . . .
11.2 I suggest that the following activities might be of benefit in the church:

12. Catering

Offers: I would like to discuss:

12.1 Helping at church functions to *a*. Provide food *b*. Prepare food *c*. Serve food *d*. Wash up *e*. And . . .
12.2 Providing hospitality to visiting preachers on Sundays

Requests:

12.1 The following refreshments/meals/kitchen equipment/and . . . would probably be of benefit to church activities:

13. Bookstall

Offers: I would like to discuss:

13.1 Serving on/helping organise the *a.* Church bookstall *b.* Library

Requests:

13.1 I suggest that the following books/literature/arrangements would be of help to me and others:

14. Office Administration

Offers: I would like to discuss:

14.1 Offering the following expertise/skills:
14.2 Offering the use of the following equipment:

Requests:

14.1 It would be of help if there were *a.* An answering phone at the manse/church office *b.* A telephone at the church *c.* A list of names, addresses and 'phone numbers of members of the church and congregation supplied to all members *d.* And . . .

15. Publicity

Offers: I would like to discuss:

15.1 Helping with *a.* Writing *b.* Editing *c.* Distributing *d.* Producing *e.* Organising church publicity material

Requests:

15.1 I would like to receive the *a.* Church magazine *b.* Weekly bulletin *c.* Minister's letter *d.* And . . .
15.2 I suggest that the following would improve the church publicity:

16. Missions

Offers: I would like to discuss:

16.1 Helping to promote missions at home and overseas by:
a. Distributing literature *b.* Serving on the missions committee *c.* Raising money *d.* Organizing prayer groups *e.* Representing the church on local committees *f.* Entertaining visiting speakers *g.* Arranging special events *h.* Preparing posters and displays *i.* Writing to missionaries *j.* And . .

Requests:

16.1 I would like to receive *a.* Missionary and denominational literature such as ______ *b.* A collecting box *c.* Information on covenanting my gifts so that income tax can be recovered for missionary and denominational support *d.* And . . .

17. Any Other Offers or Requests

SELF-APPRAISAL FORM

For Assistant Youth Club Leader

This method of self appraisal can be adapted to other tasks and leadership roles.

In column *a* give yourself marks from 1 to 5 according to how true you think the statements are of you.

If not true give yourself	0
If very slightly true give yourself	1
If slightly true give yourself	2
If moderately true give yourself	3
If largely true give yourself	4
If very largely true give yourself	5

Don't over-estimate nor under-estimate yourself!

When completed add up the marks.

If your total is:

0–22	you believe you are very poor at your job
23–44	you believe you are poor at your job
45–66	you believe you are moderately good at your job
67–88	you believe you are very good at your job
89–110	you believe you are extremely good at your job

The second column is for a friend to complete. This can be helpful – but only if you can take criticism and still remain friends!

Even if your total marks are above average, take note of those questions where low marks have been given and ask yourself what you should do to improve your effectiveness.

	a	b
1. I am fond of young people even when they behave badly		
2. I find keeping discipline quite easy		
3. Even rebellious young people usually do what I ask		
4. I feel at ease with most young people in the club		
5. I wish churches did much more for the more difficult young people		
6. I can easily hold conversations with young people		
7. The club members find it easy to be friendly with me		
8. I have done my best to encourage club members to attend church services		
9. I have been able to have serious talks about Christian things with quite a number of the club members		
10. I enjoy helping young people develop into fine Christians		
11. I enjoy joining in the fun and games with the members		
12. I am able to get on the wave-length of the young people		
13. I have found it very satisfying to work in the youth club		
14. I have behaved responsibly and reliably as assistant leader		
15. I have attended regularly and been on time		
16. The refreshment stall has been run satisfactorily		
17. I feel sorry for the young people aimlessly roaming our streets		
18. I have conducted the epilogue well		
19. I have worked well with the other leaders		
20. I have always tried to support the objectives of the club		
21. I seem to make a good job of standing in for the leader		
22. I have made the best contribution I could to decision-making when we have planned club activities		
Total		